1·50

THE FORTUNATE ISLANDS

A HISTORY OF THE ISLES OF SCILLY

A new edition
by
R. L. BOWLEY

Published by
BOWLEY PUBLICATIONS LTD   12 STATION ROAD READING

© R. L. BOWLEY, 1964

THE FORTUNATE ISLANDS
by
E. L. BOWLEY

First published	1945
2nd edition	1947
3rd edition	1949
4th edition	1957
5th edition	
revised and rewritten by R. L. BOWLEY	1964

Printed in Great Britain by
WORDEN (PRINTERS) LIMITED MARAZION CORNWALL
in 12 point Monotype Bembo on Bedford Antique Wove paper
Binding by THE PITMAN PRESS *Bath*

CONTENTS

ILLUSTRATIONS

PREFACE

THIS WORK BEGAN AS A REVISION OF "THE FORTUNATE ISLANDS: THE STORY OF THE ISLES OF SCILLY" by my father, E. L. Bowley, which was first published in 1945, and which became the standard book on the Isles of Scilly. I have now rewritten and recast the book, condensing some chapters and expanding others with fresh material. I have also included an introductory chapter for the visitor to Scilly who wishes to know something of the islands as they are today. But primarily the book is intended to be read after the "Standard Guide to the Isles of Scilly" by those who wish to know rather more of the history of the islands than the limited space in the guidebook allows.

I am most grateful to Mr. K. Sisam and to Mr. J. G. Pickwell for reading the manuscript and giving me much helpful comment and advice.

R. L. BOWLEY

The Isles of Scilly are small in size and form a relatively compact group. The map shows boat routes radiating from the island's capital of Hugh Town on St. Mary's.

INTRODUCTION: TO THE VISITOR

THE ISLES OF SCILLY CONSIST OF A GROUP OF FIVE inhabited islands[1] and over a hundred uninhabited smaller islands and rocks situated twenty-eight miles west south-west of Land's End. They are very small—the largest island, St. Mary's, is less than three miles across at its widest point and ten miles round its coastline. For the visitor in winter, Scilly offers early flowers which are the islands' principal export, and a mild climate which makes their early growth possible; in summer, the visitor can enjoy the sea, the sun, the sand and the relative solitude.

It is an advantage of small islands that they possess many times the coastline of mainland seaside resorts, and as a consequence never seem crowded. The summer visitor to Scilly can usually find an empty beach for there are so many from which to choose. The small size of the islands enables shelter to be found on a beach on a leeward shore when a stiff breeze is blowing; and the direction of the wind can be quickly determined by observing the boats at anchor in the harbour, for their prows tend to turn into the wind.

The sand on the beaches is composed of disintegrated granite, often white in colour and so fine (notably on Pentle Bay) that, when held in the palm of the hand, it will trickle through the fingers however tightly they are clenched. The sand above the high-tide line on Porthmellon was at one time considered suitable for exporting in bags and served to dry ink before blotting paper came into use.

Bathing from beaches is very pleasurable in Scilly and quite safe, with two exceptions—and then only at high tide. The two places where caution is necessary are the two sand bars, one at Porth Conger connecting the Gugh with St. Agnes, the other at Pelistry joining Toll's Island to St. Mary's. Because of the current, bathing is unsafe when the sea covers the bars. But when they are dry, the bathing is excellent on either side of the bars.

The visitor will find the sea-water rather cold for bathing, especially in the early summer, but very inviting in appearance.

[1] Strictly six if the Gugh, with one farmhouse, is regarded as separate from St. Agnes.

In sunlight the colour of the water is blue, for Scilly lies outside the boreal region where the sea teems with plankton and other microscopic organisms which, together with finely suspended mineral particles, tend to give a dull greenish hue to the sea around most of the English coast. The water around Scilly is also crystal clear because it is free from the discolouring effects of muddy rivers. When the surface is still, so transparent is the sea that the ocean floor can be observed at depths of several fathoms.

The translucency of the water round Scilly is matched by the clarity of the atmosphere free from pollution of man-made smoke and dust. The sunlight can be very bright in this area, and photographers should make some allowance for this. The strong sun helps to produce glorious colours in Scilly; but caution is advisable when sunbathing. Rash exposure of parts of the body not usually in the sun can result before very long in painful burns. The presence of a breeze sometimes lulls the unwary into a false sense of security, but salt sea air is likely only to intensify the burning. A limited amount of sunbathing is certainly beneficial to health; but it may be worth pointing out that it has been claimed that very much browning (which is nature's protection against the body absorbing too much ultra-violet) may result in a loss of ability to assimilate these rays in the following winter when they are most needed as a help in resisting ailments.

For the active visitor one of the attractions of Scilly is the large amount of open land available for walking without being obliged to tramp along tarred roads. Soft spongy turf, varied and changing views, and stimulating clambering over safe and firm granite, can form the greater part of any hike in Scilly. For so small an area it is surprising how much good walking can be obtained, though much of it should more accurately be classed as scrambling. Scilly has no high cliffs, however, and the highest point, Telegraph Hill, rises to only 159 feet above mean high water,[1] though there is scope for rock climbing particularly at Peninnis Head, St. Mary's, and at Shipman Head, Bryher. In Scilly all rock is granite which

---

[1] The Isles of Scilly were last levelled in 1887; unfortunately the documents relating to this levelling were destroyed by enemy action during the second World War. The height of the highest point of land in the Isles of Scilly can be otherwise expressed as 165 feet above mean sea level.

never crumbles under foot and, except when wet or covered with seaweed, is never slippery.

But to many visitors the primary delights of Scilly are the boat trips; not just once round the bay which is all most mainland seaside resorts can hope to offer, but adventurous expeditions to unfrequented islets to see seals, sharks and less common sea birds in their natural surroundings; or to uninhabited islands to land for the day where no other footsteps have marred the sandy bays; or to explore caves like Underland Girt on remote White Island, or Piper's Hole on Tresco; or to search Beady Pool, St. Agnes, for chocolate-coloured Venetian beads which are occasionally washed ashore from a centuries-old wreck; or to visit a distant lighthouse such as the Bishop to deliver mail or newspapers by line to the grateful keepers. It is this form of interest that gives to boating in Scilly a character all its own. Launches leave St. Mary's Quay at 10.15 a.m. and 2.15 p.m. in the summer, and in suitable weather offer a wide choice of trips.

Each of the larger islands deserves a day visit, for each has its own particular mood and charm. St. Agnes is wild and rugged on its western shores, a fitting bulwark to the elements, yet Porth Conger is one of the best bathing beaches. St. Martin's is soft and sweet-scented with panoramic views of sea, sand and heather which in strong sunlight produce breath-taking contrasts of vivid colour. Tresco with its caves, fine beaches and subtropical gardens is a common favourite; while Bryher can change from the ruggedness of Shipman Head to the placidity of Rushy Bay after a fifteen minute walk. Nor should St. Mary's be neglected, for it has much to offer: Bar Point, Watermill Bay, Pelistry, Porth Hellick, Peninnis and the Garrison are varied and all are attractive, and wherever one goes in Scilly there is a changing landscape with glorious new views.

Today the Isles of Scilly are said to form one of the most prosperous communities for its size in the British Isles. They have come a long way since the time in the last century when the inhabitants petitioned the public through the columns of *The Times* to relieve their " extreme distress ".

The basis of the prosperity of the islands in the early part of this century has been the cultivation of flowers for sale. This industry is said to have begun in about 1881 when William Trevellick of Rocky Hill Farm sent some cut flowers to Covent Garden packed in a hat box. The experiment was a financial success and the industry grew rapidly till today most suitable land is devoted to it and daffodils are the islands' glory as well as being their winter livelihood. Fortunately, flowers require little space, and even minute cottage gardens are used to augment the supply, often at the expense of vegetables and non-commercial flowers. The cultivation, packing and marketing of flowers is a skilled process. Flower farmers—they are always called farmers—have to contend with many forms of disease to which flowers are liable, with competition from East Anglian flower growers nearer the central markets who heat the ground with pipes to bring on the bulbs, and also with the daily fluctuations in prices. This requires a "know-how" out of all proportion to what seems, at first, a simple proposition. Bulbs are expensive and much capital is required to stock even a small field. There are also unpredictable changes in the buying habits of the public; today, people discriminate much more among flowers, and some of the older varieties are no longer in demand, and new varieties have had to be developed in the islands to meet the changing fashions.

A successful season also depends on the weather. A severe winter in Scilly can delay the flowers so that profits are considerably reduced; on the other hand a cold snap on the mainland, or on the continent, can have the reverse effect and bring considerable profit to Scillonian growers.

It is fortunate that the Scillonian "Year" is spread over the seasons in such a manner that there are few labour problems. In winter, and in late autumn after the storms have left sea-weed on the beaches, carts and tractors haul up the weed for subsequent use as fertilizer on the bulb fields.

From January to March, the islanders are mainly engaged in picking and packing flowers—the men pick and pack while the women bunch and tie. When the flowers are ready and the market price satisfactory, all islanders capable of lending a hand drop all other business until the packed boxes are safely on board the boat or plane on their way to market.

In May, June and July there is work in the fields. About half the bulbs must be dug up annually for separation and drying. They may also be par-boiled to destroy eel-worm, or treated to protect them from the many forms of virus to which they are susceptible. Some are refrigerated in order to accelerate their winter sleep and enable them to advance their flowering season by several days or even weeks. After planting, straw, weeds and refuse may be burnt on the surface to encourage growth.

From April to October there is a continual flow of visitors to be catered for, and from visitors comes the only other major source of income. In October, when visitors are scarce, there is a short period of relaxation before the arrival of the early flowers, and at this season many islanders will be found on the mainland or on holiday abroad.

In early autumn motor launch owners are busy in their boat houses, painting and repairing their boats for the Ministry of Transport's inspections in the coming February or March. In order to obtain a licence to take more than twelve passengers, boatmen have to submit their stripped motors to detailed inspection on the bench and later, assembled and in action, on the sea. Every craft has to conform to strict specifications.

The distinction between a " tripper "—one who comes for the day, a " visitor "—one who stays for a week or more, and a " resident "—a mainlander who has taken to living on the islands, and a " local ", is fairly clear, but not all " locals " are Scillonians. Indeed, there are said to be only some fifty families of true Scillonians—though many mainlanders have married locals and settled in the islands. Their progeny, after some generations, may lay claim to be included in the tribal ranks.   The islands would be inundated by residents, those who have retired from mainland occupations, if it were not for the severe housing shortage, and for the policy of the Duchy of Cornwall and of the Town and Country Planning Committee of discouraging indiscriminate building and giving priority to local applications for land.

The Council of the Isles of Scilly are hard put to it to find space for building houses in Hugh Town, and the exceptionally high cost of building has been a major obstacle. Since wages are on a par with those on the mainland, it has proved difficult to fix rents on an economic basis. As is inevitable in remote non self-supporting areas, the cost of living is high and nearly all the staple commodities have to be imported from Penzance, including (surprisingly) fish, meat and vegetables. An exception is milk and cream for which there is a large demand in the summer months, but there are sufficient Guernsey cows (Scilly was the first " tuberculosis free " area in the country) to cater for this.

But prices tend to be higher in Scilly than on the mainland and this is partially explained by freightage charges. The islands suffered a blow in 1954 when they were assessed for income tax for the first time in their history.

There is still a strong Nonconformist background in the islands and a " liberal " bias in political attitudes. There are five Church of England churches, two Methodist Chapels and a Roman Catholic Chapel—the Star of the Sea.

Social life, when it goes beyond the extensive family circles, may be found in the Scillonian Club, in various denominational organisations, in the Women's Institute and in music, drama, and choral societies. There are clubs for golf, football, and cricket. Dances are held throughout the year.

In the spring and summer, the Scillonians take full advantage of their opportunities for sailing and boating and there are few who do not own, or share ownership in, a motor boat or rowboat (locally called a " punt "). Although there is no fishing on a commercial scale, except the catch from lobster pots in the summer, many parties go out for pollack or mackerel. The winter brings a spate of annual dinners, including the traditional Audit Dinner for the tenants of the Duchy of Cornwall. At these functions it used to be the custom to distribute Churchwarden clay pipes.

The main interest in the islands after flowers is concerned with ships and the sea and, despite the air service to Scilly, life seems to revolve round the arrival and departure of the Isles of Scilly Steamship Company's ship. The R.M.V. Scillonian of 820 tons is licensed to carry six hundred passengers in summer, and is run by the islanders themselves, many of whom are shareholders in the Isles of Scilly Steamship Company. The voyage from Penzance takes between $2\frac{1}{2}$ and 3 hours, and nearly all supplies are brought to the island by this route. Newspapers, however, are delivered by air.

The islands are part and parcel of the Possessions of the Duchy of Cornwall, and the interests of the inhabitants are carefully safeguarded by those responsible for the administration of the Duchy. The Duchy maintains a land steward on the islands and runs an experimental farm at Trenoweth, St. Mary's. In 1949, the Duchy of Cornwall departed from its previous policy of retaining intact the freehold of all the islands. In order to afford the local Authority greater freedom under modern legislation, and particularly in housing programmes, the Duchy decided to give the sitting tenants of the properties in Hugh Town the opportunity of acquiring their houses and shops. The great majority of the tenants took advantage of the offer, about a quarter of a million pounds being paid.

The heritage of the islands as an independent and self-administered unit goes back many years. Upon the completion of the work of the Select Vestry, administrative powers for the Council to carry out its functions in relation to local government services were granted by means of Provisional Orders, from 1890 up to the date of the last Order, viz., 20th January, 1943. For local government purposes the Council of the Isles of Scilly is a County Council, Urban District, and Rural District Council. As a County Council its functions cover education, agriculture, public assistance, mental deficiency, lunacy and police. Its urban and rural powers are covered by the Public Health Acts, 1875-1936, as specifically mentioned in the Provisional Orders. Exchequer grants are received, but, after taking into account these grants, the net cost of carrying out all services in the islands has to be met from the rates.

The islands are administered by a Council composed of a chairman, four aldermen and twenty-one councillors, twelve of whom are elected from St. Mary's, three from Tresco, and two each from St. Martin's, St. Agnes and Bryher. There is a National Health Executive Council, a doctor, dentist, district nurses and a well-equipped and adequately-staffed hospital on St. Mary's. A veterinary surgeon resides on St. Mary's, and there are six justices of the peace and two policemen. Other authorities are the Royal National Lifeboat Institution; Trinity House—concerned with the lighthouses and buoys; the Coast Guards—with a station on Telegraph Hill; the Customs; and a branch office of the Ministry of Labour. There is also an Agricultural Executive.

The islands have their own Local Education Authority which administers schools on each of the inhabited islands. St. Agnes has a fluctuating number of pupils and one teacher, so have Bryher and St. Martin's. Tresco has about thirty pupils with two teachers. On St. Mary's there is one school at Carn Thomas which has just under two hundred pupils.

All ages of children from five to fifteen are catered for at Carn Thomas School except those selected for a grammar school course. The islands could not make up the numbers to justify a grammar school stream, so this type of education involves going to boarding-school on the mainland. A grant is made to cover boarding and tuition fees for those pupils selected. It was first planned to send to the mainland those left to follow a secondary modern course but, at £200 a year each, the cost was prohibitive; instead, there is a plan to build a new school on St. Mary's, but off-island children would still have to board.

In some ways for a place with less than two thousand inhabitants, the islands are exceptionally well catered for. There are some dozen or so shops and two banks (Lloyds and Barclays) on St. Mary's, and the off-islands have stores and post offices. On St. Mary's there are two public houses and a number of cocktail lounges, and there is one public house on Tresco and a licensed hotel. On St. Mary's there are five licensed hotels and several private hotels and guest houses; in addition, very many private houses provide accommodation for visitors in the season. Although the off-islands have limited scope for road traffic, there are more than two hundred assorted motor vehicles on St. Mary's, and these are exempt from Road Fund Tax, so that registration number plates are unnecessary. Drivers must, however, be covered by third party insurance and are required to hold driving licenses. An attempt has been made to institute a voluntary levy to help in the upkeep of the roads.

The outlook for the future of Scilly is bright. Forecasts that the flower trade would not be able to hold its own against competition from flower growers with better facilities nearer the markets seem to have been much exaggerated. The trade has exhibited a remarkable resilience throughout its history, and by developing new varieties, experimenting with new methods and changing to lighter flower-boxes made of cardboard instead of wood, the Scillonian farmer still sees a worthwhile future. But it is in his present spare-time pursuit of taking in visitors that his future economic prosperity seems to lie, for the accommodation which the islands have to offer is quite inadequate to cope with the number of visitors who wish to come. The danger (and all those who love Scilly are only too conscious of this) is that in developing Scilly and providing the amenities to cope with extra visitors, some of the unspoilt beauty and unique atmosphere of Scilly may be lost for ever. At present the twenty-eight miles of sea between Scilly and Land's End serves as a moat defending the naturalness of Scilly from the caravan, the touring car and the itinerant camper; and both the Council of the Isles of Scilly and the Duchy of Cornwall have been at pains to take a long term view of the well-being of the islands, and have been concerned to prevent their being spoilt by ill-judged or hasty development. But making for change are strong commercial pressures, which are only held in check by the obvious economic well-being of the islands as they are.

Whatever the outcome of the current changes in Scilly, the particular qualities of self-reliance, intelligence, industry and foresight which are most marked in Scillonians should serve them well in whatever future is in store for them in these fortunate islands.

I

THE MYTHOLOGY
The Hesperides (Isles of the Blest) and the Cassiterides
(The Tin Islands)

IN GREEK AND LATIN MYTHOLOGY FREQUENT MENTION IS made of islands situated beyond the Pillars of Hercules (Straits of Gibraltar) and called variously The Islands of the Blest, The Hesperides, the Elysian Fields, Atlantis or simply the Fortunate Islands. There the inhabitants dwelt in beautiful meadows rich with flowers and sunshine, and (according to mediaeval manuscripts) dead heroes were brought thither where they might rest and find immortality amidst perpetual summer and abundance.

The claim of the Scillies to be identified with these islands rests on Celtic origins of the story. Celtic legends and folklore refer to a land of the dead called Avalon or Glasinnis which mediaeval manuscripts say was situated in south-western Britain and referred to as the Land of Shades where peculiar sacrifices were performed, and where some islands were inhabited entirely by holy men, and where others were forbidden to men and occupied solely by women. Some substance for the view that the Scillies are the Hesperides is provided by the extraordinary number of chambered barrows of the Megalithic Period that have been found on Scilly, many more than in the whole of Cornwall, a county that is itself noted for them. These barrows or ancient burial mounds are out of all proportion to the number and style of living of persons who, according to the evidence of excavated villages, were then natives of the islands. There is reason to believe, therefore, that the graves were erected for princes (and possibly their families) of greater renown than could ever have lived and ruled locally. The relative inaccessibility of the islands would have made them a safe depository for sentimental and material treasures, and a suitable place for the remains of a departed chief to rest undisturbed and in peace. Moreover, since it was believed that the spirit of the departed could not cross water, a dead chief left on Scilly would be unable to return to his native land to embarrass his successor.

An older view of Hugh Town from Garrison Hill. Queen Victoria preferred to walk rather than ride in a coach down this steep slope.

B

Porthcressa Bay, St. Mary's, looking towards Telegraph Tower, the highest point on the islands from which the mainland can be seen on clear days.

A barrow on the Gugh is believed to be one of the earliest on Scilly. Below the cremated remains of Middle Bronze Age people, human bones from an earlier period have been found which had been inhumed. This practice of burying the body in a sitting posture, and later in a lying position, lasted till about 1700 B.C. when it was superseded by that of cremating the body first and then placing the ashes in urns often in existing barrows. From about 600 B.C. barrow construction became rare and urn fields became the rule. As has been pointed out there seems a curious anomaly in building an everlasting vault for the reception of nothing more than mortal ashes.

In addition to passage graves and covered galleries, numerous cysts or stone boxes, usually consisting of four stones set at right angles and covered by a single capstone, are still to be found on many of the islands in Scilly. There are also four monoliths or standing stones, the most impressive of which, " The Old Man of Gugh ", lies in a solitary spot on the downs of that island. Similar monoliths are found in Syria, Egypt and Brittany and their original purpose can only be surmised as connected with religious ceremonies. Before the days of parchment and written documents, ceremonies must have been essential to validate contracts. Weddings often took place at hole stones through which bride and groom clasped hands to plight their troth, and this ritual recognised and sanctified the occasion; moreover, the place and the stone would therefore be likely to acquire significance of its own by association with the event. In like manner other stones probably became places for the punishment of wrong-doers.

From pieces of pottery, funeral urns, stone mace-heads, flint instruments, holed stones, saddle querns and stone mortars which have been found in Scilly, it is clear that the islands were inhabited at least as far back as 4000 years ago. The remains of round huts dating from the Bronze Age have been discovered, and one on English Island Point, St. Martin's, has an impressive midden or refuse dump alongside, indicating clearly the diet of the early inhabitants from the great quantity of limpet shells it contains. But these relatively insignificant huts built for the living contrast strikingly with the massive masonry of the tombs built to house the dead.

The barrows were all constructed between 2500 and 4000 years ago and indicate considerable engineering skill. They were built with the use of primitive instruments only, and their construction may in some ways have resembled that which we now believe was employed in the building of Stonehenge, namely by using log rollers, levers, and considerable manpower for haulage. Splitting of the granite stones was accomplished by inserting dry wooden wedges into crevices in the sides, and then soaking them with water till the expansion of the wood split the whole stone. Many boulders on the islands still show indentations which were originally made for the wedges.

Unfortunately, quite apart from the destructive effects of weather, many of the barrows have been despoiled by local farmers looking for shaped stone for hedging and walling, and by plunderers who, particularly in the 18th and 19th centuries, opened many of the barrows seeking the jewellery and valuables which it became widely believed they contained, and which had originally been buried with the dead for their use in the next world by people who believed in the immortality of the body as well as of the spirit. Archaeologists have been fortunate in that the plunderers missed so much, for besides valuables and jewellery, tools and weapons and even food were buried, though the food soon perished.

Early man's touching concern for (and perhaps timorous fear of) those whom he had lost, and his simple faith in the continuing efficacy of earthly aids in the life beyond the grave has provided man today with a picture of his early ancestors which would otherwise have been lacking. If to the grave finds the contents of early rubbish dumps is added, a realistic commentary on the life man lived in prehistoric times is obtained—as revealing a story as an examination of the contents of present day dustbins would reveal to a future age.

For many centuries attempts have been made to settle the question whether the Scillies may reasonably be identified with the Cassiterides, those secret islands from which the Phoenicians obtained supplies of tin. These venturesome sea-traders, who reigned supreme in the Mediterranean for many centuries till about 600 B.C., came from a coastal strip of land in present-day Syria. The comparative fewness of agricultural opportunities in their homeland was one reason for the energy with which they built up a sea-borne carrying trade. From Sidon and Tyre they founded Carthage and other colonies, and Herodotus tells us that the Phoenicians starting from the Red Sea succeeded in circumnavigating Africa—and this they accomplished two thousand years before Bartholomew Diaz and Vasco da Gama found the east coast of Africa by sailing round the Cape of Good Hope from the Atlantic.

Strabo tells us that the Phoenicians sailed " beyond the Mediterranean " soon after the Trojan War (circa 1200 B.C.), and it must have been about this time that the colony of Gades (Cadiz) was founded. From here they probably voyaged northwards; but according to legend and tradition it was Melkarth, the Tyrian " Hercules," who, navigating beyond the known world to the Shades, eventually found the Cassiterides and tin.

The Phoenicians left no lasting monuments or material tokens by which their presence could be identified, and this applies equally to Mediterranean colonies in Cyprus, Crete and Sicily. One explanation is that the Phoenicians may have traded in perishable necessities, particularly food, in exchange for the tin. They almost certainly brought salt, and with the tin they obtained they are known to have made utensils and hand mirrors, and to have distilled a purple dye. There are numerous references to tin being one of the main articles of Phoenician commerce.

The evidence for any islands' being positively identified as the Cassiterides is meagre. The Phoenicians kept their source of tin a secret from everyone for over five hundred years. The mystery was so well preserved that Julius Caesar when he landed in Britain in 55 B.C. was not aware that he had come to the land " whence tin came ", although the helmets, shields and breastplates of his soldiers were made from metal of which some ten per cent. is estimated to have originated from Cornwall. The secret must have been known to the Phocian Greeks who founded Marseilles about 600 B.C. and they were the first to penetrate the secret. Strabo writing about A.D. 18 relates:

" Formerly, the Phoenicians alone carried on this traffic (tin) from Gades, concealing the passage from everyone, and when the Romans followed a certain ship master that they also might find the market, the ship master, of jealousy, purposely ran his vessel upon a shoal, leading on those who followed him into the same destructive disaster; he himself escaped by means of a fragment of the ship, and received from the Public Treasury the value of the ship and cargo he had lost. The Romans, nevertheless by frequent efforts, discovered the passage."

The earliest writers are unanimous in maintaining that the source of tin was beyond the Pillars of Hercules. Their descriptions tend in many cases towards Britain, and some specify islands whose description fits the Scillies. Herodotus, the Greek, writing in 450 B.C., whose writings go back to a period 250 years before his time, mentioned that the Cassiterides, from which the tin came, were at an extreme distance comparable with that of the source of amber from the Baltic. Strabo writing about A.D. 18 says: " The Cassiterides, opposite to the West Parts of Britain, situate as it were in the same climate with Britain, are ten in number and lie near each other, in the ocean toward the North from the haven of Artabri. One of them is desert, but the others are inhabited by men in black cloaks, clad in tunics reaching to the feet, girt about the breast, and walking with staves, thus resembling the furies we see in tragic representations. They subsist by their cattle, leading for the most part a wandering life. Of the metals, they have tin and lead, which, with skins, they barter with the merchants for earthenware, salt and brazen vessels."

Solinus states that the Tin Islands were " severed from the coast of Damnonii by a rough sea." We know that Damnonii were the inhabitants of Devon and Cornwall who later colonised Brittany in the 5th century. Pliny says " opposite to Celtiberia are a number of islands, by the Greeks called Cassiterides, in consequence of their abounding in tin."

Diodorus Siculus who lived in the first century B.C. gives an account (translated by W. Ridgeway) as follows:

" The inhabitants of that part of Britain which is called Balerium (Land's End) are very fond of strangers, and from their intercourse with foreign merchants, are civilised in their manner of life. They prepare the tin, working very carefully the earth in which it is produced. The ground is rocky, but it contains earthy veins, the produce of which is ground down, smelted and purified. They beat the metal into masses shaped like astralgi (dice) and carry it to a certain island lying off Britain called Ictis (St. Michael's Mount). During the ebb of the tide the intervening space is left dry and they carry over into this island the tin in abundance in their waggons. Now there is a peculiar phenomenon connected with the neighbouring islands, I mean those that lie between Europe and Britain, for at the flood tide the intervening passage is overflowed, and they seem like islands, but a large space is left dry at the ebb and they seem to be like peninsulas. Here then the merchants buy the tin from the natives and carry it over to Gaul and, after travelling overland for about thirty days, they finally bring their loads on horses to the mouth of the Rhone.'

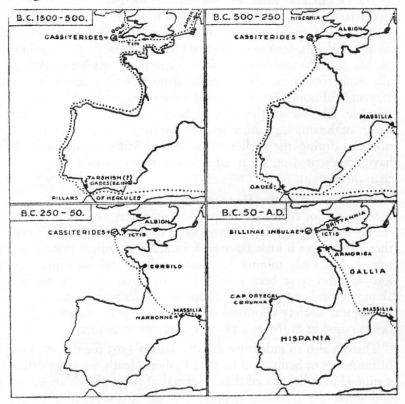

The transport of tin by sea and land throughout the centuries (conjectural)

Diodorus was writing of the traffic in his time after Gaul had been brought under Roman control. Diodorus further mentions the three sources of tin: " Tin is found in many parts of Iberia (Spain), not being discovered on the surface as some have babbled in their histories, but dug and smelted like silver and gold. For beyond the land of the Lusitanians (Portugal) are many mines of tin in the islands that lie off Iberia in the Ocean, which on this account are called the Cassiterides. And a great deal is brought from the British Island also to that part of Gaul that lies opposite; and across the midlands of the Celtic country it is brought on horseback to the people of Marseilles and to the town called Narbona."

The fact that St. Michael's Mount was used as a place of barter in the later period of the trade leads us to infer that the mainland was unsettled, and that the merchants needed the security afforded by small islands, for the protracted business of buying and selling. St. Michael's Mount, without its modern quay, was an exceptionally dangerous anchorage affording little shelter; whereas St. Ives Bay and Falmouth Estuary would seem to have been ideal for the purpose. The use of the Mount, bears witness to the turbulent nature of the times, a feature which must have been even more pronounced during the earlier traffic in tin. Scilly would probably have represented an even safer haven from general lawlessness than the Mount.

We know that the Romans used the Scillies as a place of banishment for criminals and political offenders, and there is some reason for thinking these were forced to labour in the tin mines there. But there is little trace now in Scilly of where this tin was mined. The early mining pits were shallow and therefore soon lost—it must have been one of the attractions that the tin was abundant and easy to get. There is a reference in the Royal Geological Society's Journal of 1818 to a small quantity of tin being raised in St. Mary's about twenty years before.

There is also an indenture dated as late as 1563 for the working of tin mines in Scilly, and in 1744 Robert Heath, an army officer stationed in Scilly, stated that, "several of these Islands afford tin, and some also lead and copper. The tin is discoverable by the banks next to the sea, where the marks of the ore are in some places visible upon the surface." Apparently Heath was asked by Cornish miners to make representations to the then proprietor of the islands, to obtain his lordship's consent to the working of the tin. Heath added that "a well opened in Hugh Town opposite to the landing place, that had been filled up and out of use as long as the oldest in the island ever remember, was cleaned, and when the rubbish with which it was filled was removed, the miner discovered a rich vein of tin ore, which promised encouragement for working."

There is a further deduction to be made from the fact that the range of granite radiates from Devon to the Scillies, and that tin is most plentiful on the extreme tip of Cornwall nearest to the islands. Archaeological evidence suggests that the Land's End peninsula was the most densely populated part of Cornwall from the Stone Age till late in the Bronze Age. The tin veins may have been nearer to the surface in that area than elsewhere on the mainland, and probably more exposed still in Scilly.

In time the surface tin probably became exhausted, and Cornish tin would then have been exploited—but the Scillies could have remained as the depot from which the tin was shipped to the Mediterranean and Gaul. But the whole story is lost in the mists of antiquity and Scilly's claim to positive identification with the Cassiterides remains therefore a tentative one.

II

LYONESSE AND KING ARTHUR

THE LEGEND OF THE LOST LAND OF LYONESSE AND OF A large continent, Atlantis, that once existed in the Atlantic but which was inundated by the sea, has persisted for centuries, and has inspired many poets and writers to produce immortal tales which do not pretend to be other than imaginative fantasies. Whether 140 villages with their churches once existed between Land's End and Scilly, as the legend pretends, is very doubtful; but it is certain that this shallow sea (nowhere over 300 feet deep) was once dry land, though probably not in the time of man. It is also possible that a deluge occurred, though it is more likely to have been a gradual process than a sudden cataclysm. At one time the islands were certainly much larger than today, and the rising sea drowned the valleys leaving the granite hilltops as islands. But there is no record of a calamitous event happening in Scilly in historical times, though minor inundations are likely and some coast erosion a known fact.

In 830 A.D., a thousand persons are known to have been drowned on islands near Cork in Ireland, and in the Anglo-Saxon Chronicle it is recorded that on the 11th November, 1014, " the sea-tide ran up so very high and did so much harm as no one remembered that it ever before did." In Edward the First's reign (1272–1307) there is known to have occurred an inundation at Old Winchelsea near Rye, and in the Welsh Triads there is a story of a great inundation about 500 A.D. which destroyed nineteen fortified towns in Wales. It is not difficult to imagine that these incidents may well have been part of widespread disturbances including Scilly. The Trevelyan family bears a crest commemorating an ancestor who saved himself from his Lyonesse estates at the time of an inundation by mounting a white horse which carried him to safety. Since crests have existed barely 700 years, it seems likely, if we are to believe the story, that inundations occurred within historical times, particularly as we know that erosion and subsidence have taken place in Mounts Bay within historical times. Doubtful identification of islands mentioned in mediaeval documents could well be explained if they were victims of a rising sea. Moreover the stone hedges, and foundations of buildings such as those on Par Beach, St. Martin's, which are half below the high tide line are conclusive evidence that the sea has encroached considerably within historical times, even if the legendary " drowned village " off Samson has evaded detection.

On the ten fathom line all the present islands of Scilly become hills on one large island about seven miles long and less than six miles wide, with a long narrow peninsula projecting out an additional three miles in the direction of the Bishop. Flint and chalk formations at Land's End and on Castle Down, Tresco, have been found to be exactly similar, and glacial deposits of chalk flints and greensand chert on St. Martin's are similar to the Eocene river gravels of Devon and Dorset, indicating that the islands were once part of a table-land over which rivers radiating from Dartmoor flowed outwards to the edge of the Continental shelf two hundred miles west of Scilly.

That a tract of land called Lyonesse (or, in Cornish, Lethowsow) existed as a partial or entire connection with the mainland, is an article of faith with West Cornishmen and Scillonians and as a tradition will die hard. It is embellished with an account of a great town, called the City of Lions, at the Seven Stones where the lightship is now stationed, and where the site is still spoken of as "The Town ". It is claimed that at the Seven Stones small diamond-shaped panes set in lead and forming rude casements have been found, and the tops of buildings observed under the sea. Heath states that "at Sennen Church-Town, near the extremity of Cornwall, there is the base of an old stone-column, belonging to a building, which was taken up by some fishermen, at the place of the Seven Stones, about 18 inches height and 3 feet diameter at the circular base. Besides which, other pieces of building, and glass-windows, have been taken up at different times in the same place, with divers kinds of utensils . . ." But there is no record in the Annals of Tavistock Abbey (founded 961) of any such occurrence, though St. Nicholas's Abbey may not have been attached till after 1100. Moreover, a catastrophe of such magnitude, if it occurred in historical times, would surely have been recorded from many sources. The story of Lyonesse probably gained credence from Malory's romantic story of the Knights of

the Round Table and the story of King Arthur, later also used by
Tennyson who visited Scilly for a few days on his " Arthurian
journey ". The story has inspired many poets and writers, in
Brittany as well as England, including Milton, Spenser, Dryden,
Scott, Swinburne, and William Morris. In the course of time fact
and fiction are so easily confused and so hard to disentangle. But
only the romantic will now cling to the belief in company with
Spenser that " fertile Lyonesse " really did exist once upon a
time " on the confines of faery land."

King Arthur had no chronicler, for few save priests were
literate in the sixth century. No contemporary manuscript has
come down to us to record his saga, nor even ballad or verse.
According to one account he was made King of Britain when he
was fifteen and " well beloved among all men." His story belongs
to the days when Britain belonged to the Britons and his life was
a crusade of a Christian leader fighting against the pagan Anglo-
Saxon invaders. In legend he ruled at his castle at Tintagel over all
the land of Devon, Cornwall, Lyonesse and Cassiteris (Scilly)
which latter provided the setting for the final scene of his great
tragedy. In history we hear of British princes of the name of
Arthur engaged in a noble but losing fight to stem the westward
movement of the English. At Mount Badon (about 500 A.D.)
a great battle slowed the advance for a generation. But Arthur
seems to have been active in many parts of the land which may
well indicate a composite figure built in folk tales from the
exploits of many such valiant local defenders. He is the legendary
hero of the Britons, and is said to have defended his people against
the Saxon invader, and their Christian faith against the idolatry of
Odin. He fought twelve great battles ending with that of Camlon
and was buried in Avalon at Glastonbury, though the Bretons
claim this to be in Brittany. J. C. Walters has said that "Arthur's
graves are so many that it would be easy to reduce the whole thing
to an absurdity by saying, that if there were a doubt that King
Arthur ever lived, his numerous ' graves ' conclusively prove that
he died many times, despite the tradition, too, that he did not
die at all ! "

" The name of King Arthur has been perpetuated in more
place-names and local association (says Dr. Dickinson) than any
other person, save only the devil ! " In the British Isles alone,
more than 600 localities cherish traditions of King Arthur, and

Lord Bacon remarks that " in the acts of King Arthur there is enough to make him famous, besides that which is fabulous." He is also associated with the search for the Holy Grail which, in Celtic legend, was a vessel as rich in food and as inexhaustible as the purse of Fortunatus in gold.

The final battle of his reign was against his kinsman Mordred, said to be King of the Picts and Scots: " Never (says one chronicler) was there seen a more dolefuller battle in any Christian land: for there was but rushing and riding, foining and striking, and many a grim word was there spoken either to other and many a deadly stroke. But always King Arthur rode throughout the battle of Sir Mordred many times, and did there rightly nobly as a noble king should do; and at all times he never fainted."

The Rev. H. Whitfield in his book " Scilly and its Legends " published in 1852 gives the legend of King Arthur as it concerns Scilly. He writes an imaginative account of King Arthur's followers fleeing throughout Cornwall after their King's death, pursued by Mordred and rebel Knights. After passing over the tract of country called Lyonesse, the figure of Merlin the Wizard appeared in front of Mordred and caused the earth to quake and the land to sink engulfing all the rebels, while the loyal followers of Arthur escaped safely to Scilly, there to live in peace.

> " So all day long the noise of battle roll'd
> Among the mountains by the winter sea;
> Until King Arthur's Table man by man,
> Had fall'n in Lyonesse about their Lord,
> King Arthur . . . "   TENNYSON
>   (" Morte d'Arthur ").

> "Then rose the King and moved his host by night,
> And ever push'd Sir Mordred, league by league,
> Back to the sunset bound of Lyonesse—
> A land of old upheaven from the abyss
> By fire, to sink into the abyss again;
> Where fragments of forgotten peoples dwelt,
> And the long mountains ended in a coast
> Of ever-shifting sand, and far away
> The phantom circle of a moaning sea."   TENNYSON
>   (" The Passing of Arthur ").

In the Geological Survey, by George Barrow, published by H. M. Stationery Office, it is stated that the land in this part of the world has at various periods suffered subsidence, and also elevation. It is pointed out that the sand bar called Crow Bar that lies across Crow Sound, could only have been formed at a period when the sea was at least 25 feet below its present level. This deposit dates probably from Neolithic times, since human skulls and flint implements have been found in similar circumstances elsewhere, nearly 40 feet below the present sea-level. On the other hand, the islands must have been entirely submerged in Pliocene times.

The Survey summarises the different stages:

(1)   The formation of the Old Beach, at sea-level.

(2)   The Old Beach was raised at least 40 feet.

(3)   A later subsidence "depressed the whole area of the South of Ireland, South Wales, Cornwall and the Scilly Isles at least 40 feet, for it has brought the Old Beach back again to sea-level; indeed, in the case of the Scilly Isles, almost to low-water mark."

It is, however, comforting to read the final paragraph of the Survey:

" One point has been established in the clearest manner: the area above water in the Scilly Isles has not diminished in recent times, but has distinctly increased, and this increase is due to the constant washing up of the fine sand from the shallow sea-floor to the foreshore. From this position, in dry weather, it is blown further inland and so constantly continues the process of connecting one isolated island or islet with another, and sheltering the low-lying ground behind from the inroads of the sea ".

The Scillies are therefore becoming safer and less prone to inundations by the sea. High waves which used at times to sweep across from Porthcressa to the Pool (most devastatingly perhaps on the afternoon of September 26th 1744), are now a rare occurrence owing to the raising of the high sand barrier at Porthcressa early this century. But on March 7th, 1962, a south-easterly hurricane, which caused considerable damage to the sea-wall at Old Town and swept away part of the sandbank on Par Beach, St. Martins, built up the spring tide on the 7th of the month to such a height that the sea swept across the narrow isthmus on which Hugh Town is largely situated. Breaking through the bank at Porthcressa and floating boats into the car park behind the

Town Hall, seawater flowed down the main street, flooding houses and shops, before pouring into the Pool. Happily, there was no loss of life.

An inundation of a different kind, not caused by gales, occurred in 1733 when the great earthquake at Lisbon produced a tidal wave in Scilly so that low water became for a few moments high tide. Boats formerly lying inert on their sides on dry sand were lifted bodily on the crest of the waves, straining at the limits of their anchor chains. Fortunately, the sea was calm and at low water, so little damage resulted and the sea quickly subsided.

III

ROMANS, SAXONS AND VIKINGS

THE ROMAN INVASION OF BRITAIN IN A.D. 43 BEGAN under the corpulent Emperor Claudius; for the next 400 years most of the southern part of Britain was occupied by the Romans. Unlike previous invaders, however, the Romans did not come to exterminate the inhabitants or to enslave them but to subdue and rule over them, and acquire for the Roman Empire yet another province. In this they were successful to a large extent south of the Fosse Way. North of this line was a military zone in which the " pax Romana " did not always reign, and even after the building of the massive demarcation line known as Hadrian's Wall, the Pictish barbarians to the north and Saxon pirates round the coast provided scope for constant military activity.

The area of Roman civilian settlement did not extend as far west as Cornwall so that few traces of Roman times survive, but it is probable that a military or penal establishment was kept in Scilly since there are records of the islands being used as a place of banishment. The Emperor Maximus transported " Instantius ", a bishop of Spain, to Scilly for heresy in the time of Priscillianus, anno 380, and the Emperor Marcus banished a false prophet during the time of the rebellion of Cassius for, " pretending to prophesy, and foretelling of things to come, as if he was inspired ", and sent him to the " Silia Insula ".

In 1950, excavation on Par Beach, St. Martin's, just above the high tide line, revealed the foundations of two clearly defined round houses a few feet below the sand, together with pottery of Roman influence and two fragments of Samian ware. Tradition maintains that a " Roman causeway " existed joining St. Martin's to St. Mary's along the top of Crow Bar. This " road " is more likely to have been a stone " hedge " round the fields that undoubtedly surrounded the houses on Par Beach and possibly others yet to be discovered. At low tide, a careful look at the rocks on Par Beach stretching seawards, often in remarkably straight lines, certainly confirms the impression of stone hedges.

But in support of the causeway theory it has been claimed that a possible continuation of the "Roman Road" can be found from Bar Point on St. Mary's, and some Scillonians claim that their grandparents remembered seeing large flat stones on the bar at low spring tides. No sign of flat stones can be seen today but the shifting sand could well have covered these. If so, it is remarkable that if they are of Roman origin they should have been covered only within the last two generations.

With the exception of a few Roman coins found in Scilly, a possible Roman altar, a reference to Scilly ling being regarded as a delicacy, and Strabo's accounts of the tin trade and of the visit of Publius Crassius who observed the tin being mined, little is known of Scilly in the Roman period. But in 1962 some important finds were discovered just above the high tide mark on the small uninhabited island of Nornour in the Eastern Isles. These included dated Roman coins, brooches, pieces of pottery, fragments of a stone statue, and part of the stone wall of a house together with a stone fire-place. Such contact as the inhabitants of Scilly may have had with the Romans during the period of their occupation was at any rate ended in the 5th century A.D., when the Romans withdrew to defend the heart of the Empire from the invading barbarian pressure from Eastern Europe. The Britons who had become unwarlike in outlook enjoying the benefits of Roman law and Roman military protection now lay defenceless, and Britain presented a rich and tempting prize for pirates. Even before the Romans withdrew there had been plundering raids on the east and south coasts of Britain, and in the next four hundred years we know little of the Scillies except that they formed a base for marauders.

The Anglo-Saxon invasion of Cornwall (West Wales) began in 814 but it is not known when they reached Scilly. In 928 King Athelstan is supposed to have embarked with his fleet at Whitsand near Plymouth and to have subdued Scilly.[1] He is said to have left a garrison, though nothing further is heard of it, and the Collegiate Church of St. Buryan in Cornwall is said to have been founded by Athelstan as a thank-offering. Later, as a result of the arrival of the monks, the islands adopted Christianity

[1] This story has been questioned. Some believe Scilly to have been confused with somewhere else.

and an abbey to St. Nicholas was founded on Tresco. St. Nicholas as the patron saint was an appropriate choice since he was said to be able to preserve vessels from the perils of the sea if his aid was fervently invoked. St. Nicholas was Archbishop of Myra, a city of Lycia in Lesser Asia, where he died in 342 A.D. His relics (now in Bari in Italy) were said to perform miraculous cures particularly with young infants.

Into this refuge of holy men on Scilly, in about the year 980 A.D., there came nearly a hundred ships of a marauding armada of Northmen who during the previous four years had been harrying, burning, and slaughtering round the coasts of the British Isles. This great host was led by Olaf Tryggvason, King of Norway, Sweden, Denmark and Iceland, and the following is the account of Snorri Sturluson, written *circa* 1222, of events that are estimated to have taken place in the year 980, and translated by William Morris and Eiriker Magnusson. The story is from what is now called the " Heimskringla " (The Round World), and is one of the best-known Sagas of the old Norse kings.

" Olaf Tryggvason was three winters in Wendland; and then Geira, his wife, fell sick, and that sickness brought her to her bane. Such great scathe did Olaf deem this that he had no love for Wendland ever after. So he betook him to his warships, and fared yet again a-warring; and first he harried in Friesland, and then about Saxland, and so right away to Flanders. Then sailed Olaf Tryggvason to England, and harried wide about the land; he sailed north all up to Northumberland, and harried there, and thence north-away yet to Scotland, and harried wide about. Thence sailed he to the South-isles, and had certain battles there; and then south to Man, and fought there, and harried also wide about the parts of Ireland. Then made he for Bretland, and that land also he wasted wide about, and also the land which is called of the Kymry; and again thence sailed he west to Valland, and harried there, and then sailed back east again, being minded for England, and so came to the isles called Scillies in the Western parts of the English Main.

" Olaf Tryggvason was four winters about this warfare, from the time he fared from Wendland till when he came to Scilly.

" Now when Olaf Tryggvason lay at Scilly he heard tell that in the isle there was a certain sooth-sayer who told of things not yet come to pass; and many men deemed that things fell out as

The harbour of New Grimsby, Tresco, showing also some of the small flower fields sheltered from winter gales by high hedges of escallonia, pittosporum or veronica.

A flower field of daffodils on St. Mary's.

"Continuous as the stars that shine   Along the margin of a bay;
And twinkle on the milky way,   Ten thousand saw I at a glance,
They stretched in never-ending line   Tossing their heads in sprightly dance."

he foretold. So Olaf fell a-longing to try the spaeing of this man, and he sent to the wise man him who was fairest and biggest of his men, arrayed in the most glorious wise, bidding him say that he was the king; for hereof was Olaf by then become famed in all lands, that he was fairer and nobler than all other men. But since he fared from Garth-realm, he had used no more of his name than to call him Oli, and a Garth-realmer. Now when the messanger came to the sooth-sayer and said he was the king, then got he this answer: ' King art thou not; but my counsel to thee is, that thou be true to thy king.'

" Nor said he more to the man, who fared back and told Olaf thereof; whereby he longed the more to meet this man, after hearing of such answer given; and all doubt fell from him that the man was verily a sooth-sayer. So Olaf went to him, and had speech with him, asking him what he would say as to how he should speed coming by his kingdom, or any other good-hap.

" Then answered that lone-abider with holy spaedom: 'A glorious king shalt thou be, and do glorious deeds; many men shalt thou bring to troth and christening, helping thereby both thyself and many others; but to the end that thou doubt not of this mine answer, take this for a token: Hard by thy ship shalt thou fall into a snare of an host of men, and battle will spring thence, and thou wilt both lose certain of thy company, and thyself be hurt; and of this wound shalt thou look to die, and be borne to ship on shield; yet shalt thou be whole of thy hurt within seven nights, and speedily be christened thereafter.'

" So Olaf went down to his ship, and met unpeaceful men on the way, who would slay him and his folk; and it fared with their dealings as that lone-abiding man had foretold him, that Olaf was borne wounded on a shield out to his ship, and was whole again within seven night's space.

" Then deemed Olaf surely that the man had told him a true matter, and that he would be a soothfast soothsayer, whence-soever he had his spaedom. So he went a second time to see this sooth-sayer, and talked much with him, and asked him closely whence he had the wisdom to foretell things to come. The lone-dweller told him that the very God of christened men let him know all things that he would, and therewithal he told Olaf many great works of Almighty God; from all which words Olaf yeasaid the taking on him of christening; and so was he christened with all his fellows.

" He abode there long and learned the right troth, and had away with him thence ' priests and other learned men'.

" In the autumn-tide sailed Olaf from the Scillies to England. He lay in a certain haven there, and fared peacefully, for England was christened, as he was now christened."

King Olaf carried his new creed to Norway, Sweden, Denmark and Iceland and enforced it at the point of the sword.

> " *King Olaf from the doorway spoke:*
> ' *Choose ye between two things my folk,*
>   *To be baptised or given up to slaughter!* ' "
>
> LONGFELLOW

Later we hear, that in Scilly, in A.D. 1155 one Svein Ashlifarson, " King of Orkney and Caithness ", raided St. Mary's and " took much plunder ". Christianity may first have found its way to Scandinavia from Scilly by way of Olaf, but plundering remained an economic necessity for Northmen.

IV

THE MONKS AND THE MIDDLE AGES

B Y THE TIME OF KING EDWARD THE CONFESSOR (WHO ruled England from 1042 to the momentous year of 1066), there was a Priory at Tresco dedicated to St. Nicholas, and a church on St. Helen's of earlier foundation. There are records of cells and chapels bearing various names on other parts of the islands.

All these religious houses eventually came under the control of Tavistock Abbey in the time of Henry I (1100–1135). The ownership of the islands of St. Elid's (St. Helen's), St. Sampson (Samson), St. Theona (Teän), Rentmen (presumably Tresco), and Nurcho or Nullo (unidentified) were included in the grant, together with all wrecks except whole ships. (In these grants gold, whale, scarlet cloth, fur and masts were always reserved for the King). In another grant all the tithes of Scilly were confirmed to the monks by Richard deWick " for his soul and the souls of his parents, and of Reginald, Earl of Cornwall, his Lord". Richard de Dunstanville, a natural son of Henry I, was created Earl of Cornwall in 1140 and confirmed the original grant to Tavistock Abbey, from which it appears that the islands were then held as part of the Earldom.

From the time of its establishment to the Dissolution of the Monasteries in 1539, the monastic community of Tresco was controlled at different times by thirty-eight Abbots. We know little of their affairs. The traces of the Abbey which are still in existence on Tresco indicate that it was of some considerable size, but the record of its final destruction is missing. We can but surmise from the evidence of charred timber that it was at some period destroyed by fire. Today the major relic is a fine Norman archway standing among the foundations of the Abbey ruins.

In a Return of Edward I's Commissioners of 1275 for the Hundred of Penwith (which included Scilly) it is stated that: " They (the Jury) say that John de Allet and the Prior of St. Nicholas (Tresco), Lords of Scilly, take wreck of the sea in those

Islands, but they know not by what warrant, the ancestors of the aforesaid John and the Prior having done so from the time whereof memory is not." And later in Edward I's reign we find the Abbot of Tavistock claiming " all shipwrecks happening in all the Islands (i.e. the monk's islands), which he and his predecessors had enjoyed without interruption from time immemorial."

The monks must have been sorely harassed by marauders from the sea since the Civil Authority would not, or more probably could not, give the islands adequate protection. We find the monks complaining of the rigours of their existence on the islands and petitioning to be redrafted to the parent abbey at Tavistock. Possibly a tour of duty on Scilly was regarded as a disciplinary measure or penance. In the reign of Edward III (1327–1377) only two monks appear to have been resident at Tresco; and in the wars against France only secular priests were stationed in Scilly.

The following document, translated from the Norman-French, gives an interesting side-light on the Scillies as a resort and refuge of fugitive serfs in the time of Edward III. " Edward the (Black) Prince, etc. to Walter Hull, Constable of the Castle and Keeper of the Isles of Scilly: At the suggestion of our well-beloved Ralph Vyvyan, one of our tenants in Cornwall, we command you that whereas Robert Martyn, Roger Tregarn, Robert Carngonel, and others his born serfs have run away out of his seignory in Cornwall as far as the said Isles, and now remain there. We command that if it be so, you permit that he take them again, and cause them to return to his seignory as Law and Right require, and do not make any disturbance or maintenance by them against him in this matter to his disinheritance. Done under our Privy Seal at London, the 4th February, 27 Edward III."

In the Register of Bishop Grandison, dated 21st September 1351, mention is made of the impoverishment occasioned to the said Abbey (Tavistock) from the enormous devastation recently committed by Pirates in Insula de Sully—" ex qua non modica pars subsidii Monasterii de Tavistock provenire consuerit ".

Secular authority in the islands was vested in the Earls of Cornwall by the time of Henry I, but it is not always easy to draw a distinction between ecclesiastic and secular affairs. One of the earliest known records is that of Pope Celestin III in 1193 confirming to the Abbey of Tavistock its privileges and properties, and amongst them, within the Isles of Scilly, the Isle of St.

Nicholas (Tresco), St. Sampson, St. Elidius, St. Theona the Virgin, and an island called Nutho (Nurcho) with their belongings, and all churches and oratories in all the isles, with tithes and offerings, besides two bits of wooded land in Aganus (Hagness, now St. Agnes) and three in Ennor (now St. Mary's). The rest of Scilly was a Feudal Lordship appurtenant and owing allegiance to the Castle of Launceston, and the Tenant owed suit and paid yearly a rent called "waiternfee" (or "Watching Fee") at Michaelmas at the Gate of the Castle.

The date of the building of Ennor Castle is uncertain, but it probably commenced in the time of Henry III (1216–1272) and may have been in existence earlier; it is mentioned specifically in a document dated 1244. This castle, of which little remains, has been identified as Old Town Castle and was situated in a commanding position close to what was then the main town. Its name, Ennor or Ynnor, was the secular name for St. Mary's.

In A.D. 1248, Dreux de Barrantine was sent to Scilly by Henry III to act as Governor and to administer justice. He received lands to the value of £10 in payment. The noble Norman Barrantines were a maritime family who kept as long as they could to the sea coast, and who already held the Channel Islands under the Crown. Their garrison at Ennor Castle would appear to have consisted of armed men supplied by tenants as a condition of holding land.

Edward I granted the Castle of Ennor in Scilly to Ranulph Blancminster[1] in return for finding twelve armed men, at all times to keep the peace, and paying yearly at Michaelmas three-hundred puffins, or six and eightpence. This rent of 6s. 8d. seems to have been paid yearly up to the time of Edward VI (1547), but always in the form of money.

In the year 8 Edward II (1314–1315) Ranulph Blancminster had licence to crenellate the castle. The Caption of Seizin preserved in the Duchy Office states that when the Black Prince took possession of his Duchy, the Lord of the " Manor of Scilly " was at that time Ranulf Blancminster who died Midsummer, 1348, leaving as his heir his grandson Gandewen, a minor of about nine years of age. The Duchy held the Manor during the minority, and after an interval the Black Prince granted its custody and the wardship of the heir to William of Morier, or Morrers.

1 Otherwise known as Ranulph de Blankminster or Ralph Blanchminster.

In the Minister's Accounts for the year 1348-49, the collection of rents by the Duchy is recorded. The rents collected were from bond and free tenants, perquisites of court, heriots and rent for ships calling at the islands, and a note is appended that the collection was " no more, because the great part of the Fishermen have died this year by the Pestilence."

A further account of the same Roll states that " The Yearly Rents of 100s for the Wine Tavern (Taberna vini, possibly a wine booth or Custom House) and of 40s for the Windmill were not forthcoming because both tenements had been destroyed by the Foreigners."

In 1342, six-hundred Welshmen were sent to Brittany on the King's Service, and no doubt fought later at Crécy. We learn about them, not from a Writ of Array, but from a petition of the Lord of the Isles of Scilly (Patent Rolls) setting forth that " whereas these Welshmen were drawn by the sea on to that Island staying there for 20 days and carrying away £500 worth of crops, the Tenants are not able to till their lands and pay their dues ". Whilst becalmed they had apparently plundered Scilly unmercifully.

From the Inquisition Post Mortem of the 22nd year of Edward III, it appears that " Ranulf of Blancminster held in his demesne as of fee of the Lord Edward Prince of Wales, Duke of Cornwall and Earl of Chester as of the Honour of His Castle of Launceston, the Castle of Scilly with the Islands belonging to the said Castle by Knight Service at a yearly rent of 300 puffins or half a mark. The which Castle with the islands aforesaid are worth yearly in all issues according to the true value £18 19s. 4½d."

Puffins could be eaten in Lent and would appear to have been valued for their feathers as much as their edible qualities. The normal value of puffins seemed to have increased, for, instead of 6s. 8d. or 300 puffins, in the year 1440 it was 6s. 8d. or 50 puffins. This Blancminster seems to have been a high-handed individual who, according to William le Poer,[1] Coroner on St. Mary's, instead of keeping the peace, entertained rogues, thieves and felons, and with their help committed many abuses. For this complaint Edward I appointed a commission, but nothing came of it, and William le Poer was thrown into prison by Blancminster at Le Val (probably Holy Vale) and made to pay one hundred marks.

[1] He may have had a private quarrel with Ranulf which influenced his reports.

Justice was rough in those days, for instance:—

" John de Allet and Isabella, his wife, hold the Isles of Scilly, and hold there all kinds of pleas of the crown throughout their jurisdiction and make indictments of felonies. When anyone is attained of any felony, he ought to be taken to a certain rock (that on which ' The Bishop ' now stands), in the sea, with two barley loaves and one pitcher of water upon the same rock, they leave the same felon until by the flowing of the sea he is swallowed up."

We have another reference to the administration of the Blancminsters, in this case probably that of his son and successor, John de Albo Monasterio, Knight, and M.P. for the County of Cornwall, in the year 37 of Edward III (1363–1364). In 1367 the priory of St. Nicholas having complained that " for want of proper protection it was wasted and impoverished by the frequent arrival of the seaships of all nations," King Edward III, " holding it in great esteem as a royal foundation, commands all dukes, earls, admirals, soldiers, masters of ships, and mariners, and especially the constable of his castle in the isle of Ennor to extend to the prior, monks, chaplains and their servants, all possible protection, so that they may be able to bear their proper burdens and offer prayers and devotions continuously for the King, his progenitors, and his heirs, as they had been wont to do ".

The Blancminsters were succeeded by the Coleshills, and St. Agnes was held by the Hamely family for a considerable length of time, apparently as inferior grantees. On March 25th, 1351, Ralph Hamely granted to his brother, Laurence, the " Isle of St. Agnes in Scilly, with the rents and services of the same, consisting of dried fish and wrecks of the said Island, paying yearly for seven years to come one grain of wheat and after that time one hundred shillings Sterling."

William of Worcester in his Itinerary of 1478 mentions the islands, and Richard III ordered an inquisition of them to be taken in 1484 when it appears that they were worth in time of peace, forty shillings, but in time of war—nothing! This latter value was recognition of the difficulty and danger of holding Scilly in time of war, and of the expense which it entailed.

The next important record is taken from the notes of John Leland, the antiquarian, who visited Scilly shortly after the accession of Edward VI, in 1538, but who was prevented, owing to loss of his reason, from arranging them. Some of his notes are of interest:

"St. Mary Isle is a five miles or more in cumpace, in it is a poor town, and a meately strong pile (Ennor Castle); but the roves of the buildings in it be sore defacid and worne.

"Iniscaw longid to Tavestoke, and ther was a poor cell of Tavestoke. Sum caulle this Trescaw; it is the biggest of the islettes, in cumpace 6 miles or more.

"S. Agnes Isle so caullid of a chapel theryn.

"The Isle of S. Agnes was desolated by this chaunce in recenti hominum memoria. The hole numbre of V. housholdes that were yn this isle cam to a mariage or a fest in S. Mary Isle, and going homewarde were all drownid.

"Few men be glad to inhabite these islettes, for al the plenty, for robbers by sea that take their catail by force. The robbers be Frenchmen and Spaniardes.

"One Danvers a gentilman of Wilshir whos chief house at Daundsey, and Whitington, a gentilman of Glocestreshire be owners of Scylley; but they have scant 40 marks (£26 13s. 4d.) by yere of rentes and commodities of it.

"Ther is one isle of the Scylleys cawled Rat Isle, yn which be so many rattes that yf horse, or any other lyving beast be brought thyther, they devore him. Ther is a nother cawled Bovy Isle."

The notes are very inconsistent and would appear to have been written down on a hurried visit.

With the dissolution of the monasteries, Tavistock Abbey became Crown property, but the islands are not mentioned in the records. It is clear, however, that the condition of the islands had degenerated, although £6,000 had been expended by Edward VI (1547–1553) on fortification of which little trace remains. The only use to which the islands were put—according to a bill of attainder brought against Lord Admiral Seymour in 1549—was as a pirate base. Seymour was accused of entering into relations with pirates and " to have gotten into his hands the strong and dangerous isles of Scilly where he might have a safe refuge if anything for his demerits should be attempted against him ". For this, and other matters, he was attainted and beheaded, and the islands reverted to the Crown (5th March, 1549).

V

THE GODOLPHINS, STAR CASTLE
AND THE CIVIL WAR

BY ELIZABETH'S REIGN THE CONNECTION OF THE Godolphin family with Scilly had been well established. Till the 13th year of her reign, William Godolphin, and later Thomas Godolphin, had been military governors of Scilly under the Crown. In 1571, Elizabeth leased the islands to Francis (afterwards Sir Francis) Godolphin, for thirty-eight years on condition that he defended them and paid a yearly rental of £10 to the Receiver of the Duchy.[1] Subsequent leases were granted to the Godolphin-Osborne family at £40 per annum, and for some 250 years (except during the Protectorate) they were the owners of the islands, Thereafter, for a further 31 years from 1800, the islands were leased by the representative of the Godolphins, the Duke of Leeds, who in 1831 refused to renew the lease.

Shortly after the defeat of the Spanish Armada in 1588, Queen Elizabeth ordered Star Castle to be built on St. Mary's at the expense of the Crown, partly as a precaution against a further descent from Spain and partly as a protection from pirates and privateers. The Spaniards had a base at Brest, from whence issued the four galleys in 1595 which raided Mousehole and Penzance, and there was good reason to anticipate that Spain might use Scilly[2] as a base from which to launch an invasion of the mainland. The war continued till 1604, and several further Spanish invasion fleets were planned but never reached England's shores. But the danger from Spain helps to explain Elizabeth's

---

[1] This lease was opposed unsuccessfully by Mr. Edward Barkley, who asserted that Lord Admiral Seymour had purchased only the land held by Danvers, and that he, as residuary legatee of Whittington, was entitled to the castle as a part of the islands that had been wrongfully seized by the Admiral.

[2] *Cal. State Papers, Domestic, Elizabeth* 1591, *May*, 17.
Memorial (by Lord Burghley) for Sir Walter Raleigh to send a pinnace from Plymouth to Lord Thomas (Howard) to warn him of the Spaniards being about Scilly; for Darrell to provide two months' victuals for the Queen's ships, to send Sir Walter Raleigh westward with a commission to take up shipping and men to save Scilly, if not taken, and defend the coasts of Cornwall and Devonshire.

anxiety to fortify Scilly. It is on record that Philip of Spain instructed his Admiral Menandez, as early as 1574, to seize the Isles of Scilly and establish a base there; but plague broke out in the fleet, the Admiral dying of it, and the scheme was abandoned.

The rendezvous of the Armada of 1588 was Scilly, and there are many references in the State papers regarding Spain's intentions regarding the islands. The following extract from the " General Orders " issued by the Duke of Medina Sidonia, C.-in-C. of the Spanish Armada, is of interest:

" May, 1588 . . . on leaving Cape Finisterre the course will be to the Scilly Isles, and ships must try to sight the Islands from the South, if ships get separated from the Armada they are to continue on the course. If on arrival there the Armada is behind them, they will cruise off the place until the Armada appears . . . "

As a consequence of the Menandez episode, the attention of Elizabeth and her advisers was directed to Scilly, and Francis Godolphin was ordered to conduct an enquiry.

In the Calendar of State Papers (Eliz. I. add: 1579) his reply is given, and some details are of special interest as showing the condition of the isles at that time.[1]

"(1) The rent of £20 is paid to the Queen for the islands, and she is at no charge, except that she sometimes grants an allowance for powder.

(2) As to Abbey lands, Treskawe Island belonged to Tavistock Abbey, and Chris. Coplestone can shew writings for Brear Island. Mr. Fortescue for Agnes Isles, and the heirs of Mr. Whittington and Mr. Danvers for others. No ancient rents were paid except puffins or like small value.

(3) King Edward VI built two clock houses (blockhouses) in St. Mary's Isle and began a fort and a house, and two clockhouses on Treskawe, their charge, with that of the garrison, cost £6,000.

(4) Lord Admiral Seymour not only had the Abbey lands, but all the Islands, buying the interests of others.

(5) Since the Islands came into King Edward's possession, 80 tenements have been erected and laborious inclosures of rough land made.

---

[1] Quoted from an article by J. E. Hooper in the Journal of the Old Cornwall Society.

(6)   There are now not a hundred men, but more women and
children; the tillable ground does not find half of them
bread. Only the two islands wherein are fortifications are
inhabited; two others are habitable for 20 persons. There
are good roads (*anchorages*) and convenient harbours, and
it would be mischievous for the enemy to take them; but
I could not defend them in war, without help."

In the Calendar of State Papers appear the following:

"Aug. 9th, 1587. The Council to Sir George Carey. Report of
a fleet of 120 sail having been seen off the Isles of Scilly, supposed
to be Spaniards."

"June 23rd, 1588. Information by Sir Francis Godolphin. Of
the discovery of the Spanish fleet off the Scilly Islands. Nine sail
of great ships between Scilly and Ushant, their sails all crossed over
with a red cross. English boats chased and fired at."

"July 6th, 1588. Lord Adm. Howard to Walsygham . . . Part
of the Spanish fleet had been discovered off the Scilly Islands, but
they had been dispersed by the stormy weather."

The Spanish Armada was defeated in 1588 and with the his-
torians hindsight can be seen to mark the beginning of the
decline of Spanish power. But to contemporaries, Spain was still
the greatest power on earth and her fleets " marvellously strong."
A further Armada might be expected to be launched against
England's shores and was to be prepared for. In 1593, Queen
Elizabeth, usually so indecisive, finally made up her mind and
Sir Francis Godolphin received the following letter dated 9th
May, 1593:

" Having resolved upon fortifying St. Mary's Island according
to a plan which will be brought to him, order will be given that
£400, the estimated charge, be delivered to him of the revenue
of that County (Cornwall) as required for keeping such fort and
two other sconces. During the summer a lieutenant, three
gunners, and twenty-six soldiers are appointed, whose wages
will amount to £1 1s. 10d. a day or £30 11s. 4d. a month, but
thinks only ten soldiers are necessary in winter.

" He is to see that some of the inhabitants of St. Mary's assist
the said retinue if required; has ordered according to his request
four iron demi-culverins to be sent, authorises him to send two
minions of brass, which are in his custody in Cornwall; he will

order powder and bullets for the pieces, and matches, muskets, pikes, and halberts for the Garrison. He is to undertake the building of the fort, with advice of Robert Adams, and to choose the persons to guard it, using circumspection for avoiding superflous charges.

" Upon knowing from him in what part of Cornwall, next to the Isles, some convenient number may be put in readiness to resort to the Isle upon any great necessity, order shall be given therefor."

The building of Star Castle is a very good and characteristic example of how well Queen Elizabeth was served by her subjects, and how parsimonious was her administration in the matter of rewards. Speed was essential—threatening Spanish vessels were frequently seen near the coast—and Robert Adams must have been a genius, since the whole building, commenced in June, 1593, was completed by December, 1594. Not only was the work well and truly done, but he found time to incorporate certain decorations, and never for one instant did he fail to preserve those superb proportions that distinguished the best architecture of the period. He received, for his services, 13s. 4d. a day. Up to December, 1594, the cost had reached £958 11s. 2d., of which only £450 had been paid, and although approved at the time, the extra expenditure incurred by Sir Francis was not paid until November 24th, 1603—nine years after its presentation.

The following is taken from the Calendar of State Papers. Domestic—Elizabeth VCCXLV. 72:

"August 6th, 1593.

Sir Fras. Godolphin to Lord Burghley. Adams is well deserving, for besides his perfect skill in numbers and measures, he is very provident in saving, and no less painful in attending; the work considered, so much has seldom been performed at such small charge, and with so few hands in so short a time."[1]

Star Castle was built in 1593 on the high rocky peninsula joined to the main part of St. Mary's by a sandy isthmus on which Hugh Town now stands. Some of the stones from Ennor Castle are believed to have been used in its construction, and many of the inhabitants of Old Town moved for greater protection as near to

---

[1] The last sentence of Sir Francis Godolphin's report is reminiscent of Sir Winston Churchill's speech in 1940 on the nation's debt to the pilots of Fighter Command.

the new fortress as possible. The quay at Hugh Town, which was later extended, was built in 1601 and Hugh Town has been the metropolis and port of the islands ever since.

Star Castle (Stella Mariae) takes its name from the star form of the plan; certain of its salients recall the walled cities of Flanders; at the time that it was built, although small, it was rivalled only by Upnor Castle and Tilbury Fort. The two-storied residence, which conforms to the general stellar plan, is surrounded by eighteen-foot granite ramparts on which is a skirting wall with numerous embrasures for muskets and cannon. On the ramparts are four small rooms in each of which a captain of the garrison was lodged, each being privileged to dine at the Governor's table. Over the entrance are the initials E.R. (Elizabeth Regina) and below are R.A. (probably Robert Adams or possibly Sir Ramfrye Arundel) and F.G. (Francis Godolphin). The arched entrance, which could be closed by a portcullis, is surmounted by a bell tower, and there is an embrasure for a cannon to command the approach. Close alongside is a sally-port leading to the dry moat which surrounds the castle. The original roof was of thatch.

Carew says: " Sir Francis Godolphin reduced the place to a more defensible plight, and by his invention and purce bettered his plot and allowance, and therein so tempered strength with delight and both with use, as it serveth for a sure Hold and commodious Dwelling."

In the Calendar of State Papers there are notes by Sir Francis Godolphin on the importance of keeping the Isles of Scilly:
" Scilly lies 30 miles from the Land's End of Cornwall W.S.W., being the nearest port of Her Majesty's dominions towards Spain. It is as an inn by which ships trading Westerly or Southerly are to pass and return, whereby it both succours and secures our traffic, and no other place can so aptly permit or restrain the traffic of Ireland and the north of Scotland with France and Spain. The enemy may soon make it impregnable and use it as a rendezvous with his Navy, a citadel or scourge against the realm . . . proving a more hurtful neighbour in the West than Dunkirk is in the East. Neither Falmouth nor Plymouth which have the country's strength always ready to reinforce their garrisons, deserve so strong a guard as Scilly, for

those isles cannot be reinforced, being so far distant from the main. In the reign of her Majesty's brother, they were kept by my father against the French with a guard of 150 men when Falmouth had but 10. I will offer £500 towards the charges needful for the fortification if Her Majesty would grant me such further term in those Isles as she did to my uncle . . ."

In 1637, it was reported that the garrison at Star Castle consisted of twenty-five men, with twenty-five more sent from the mainland for six months in the year. But at the same time the islanders could not muster more than thirty persons able to carry arms. In 1642 the garrison in Scilly had increased to 165 men and the cost of maintenance to £261 per month.

The first distinguished visitor to Star Castle was Prince Charles, afterwards Charles I, who together with his and his father's favourite, George Villiers, Duke of Buckingham, and Captain Henry Mainwaring, landed in Scilly in September, 1623, and stayed for four nights. They were returning from Spain after an unsuccessful and unpopular attempt to arrange a marriage between Charles and the Spanish Infanta. It is not clear why the ships put into Scilly but there would appear to have been some discord on board the fleet of a nature which determined the Prince that he would land.

The following account is taken from the Navy Records:
" On Sunday, September 21, a Council of War was held on the ' Prince Royal ', at which the possibility of landing the Prince on one of the Isles of Scilly in a ketch was discussed. For this purpose several pilots had put off from the islands, but by the time they reached the flagship, the idea had been postponed. However, after supper the matter was again debated, and beyond expectation, order was given to make ready the longboat and to call the ketch, and the Prince made choice of the company that were to accompany him to the shore.
"About one of the clock after midnight, with great danger to his Highness' person and to the Duke of Buckingham, they were put into our longboat, which was veered astern by a long warp, where the ketch, laying the longboat on board, and the sea going somewhat high, they entered the ketch disorderly, without regard to any, but everyone shifting for himself.
" Being all shipped, the ketch was so overburdened as she could

make but little way, so that after we had taken farewell with a discharge of a volley of our great ordinance, we tacked into the sea.

"After six hours' buffeting the ketch succeeded in making St. Mary's Island where the Prince and his retinue landed. The flagship being now for the time bereft of the services of her Captain and also the Master, Walter Whiting, the Earl of Rutland, Commander of the Fleet, held a council on board to decide what course it would be advisable to take. After serious consultation with two pilots of the island it was agreed that the ' Prince Royal ' (flagship) might go into the roadstead without danger.

" We came to anchor in the best of the roadstead about two of the clock afternoon, the Prince and all his train standing upon the lower point of the land, and welcomed us in as we passed close by, with much expression of joy and heaving up their hats."

The writer of the above record indicates very clearly that this visit " beyond expectation " and involving a stormy and dangerous six hours' voyage in an overburdened ketch at one o'clock in the morning, was not encouraged by the naval experts, but he does not state what motive induced the Prince to visit the islands in such a hurry and in such an unceremonious manner. On leaving Star Castle the Prince gave Sir Francis Godolphin " a chayne of gold to the value of £50 and many other large giftes ".

The family of Godolphin suffered a severe tragedy in October, 1636. The Egmont papers contain the following letter:

" Edmund Percival to Sir Phillip Percival.

" I advise you to send no cattle over to Ireland whilst the Turks are so busy, lest both your cattle and your gentlemen should suffer, there having been a multitude of passengers taken this summer. Sir Francis Godolphin and his lady, and his servants, and his brother, Captain Godolphin, and his wife, going to the Isles of Scilly some three or four leagues off the shore, were taken by the Turks, and one of the Turks attempting to abuse the Captain's wife, he presently ran him through whereupon they cut him in a hundred pieces, and they carried Sir Francis and the rest away captives. God of His mercy send us some relief ".

In 1635 no fewer than twenty sail of "Turkish" men-of-war were reported off the Scillies. They were intercepting the fishing fleet on its return from Newfoundland, and many complaints of such happenings are recorded in the State Papers of the period. These pirates (Turks, Moors, Algerians, and the Sallee Rovers) were not finally suppressed until 1816 when Sir Edward Pellew, with English and Dutch ships, bombarded and destroyed the town of Algiers.

There are, in existence, fragments of letters written by a Francis Godolphin, of the family of Sir Francis, and probably father of the famous Sydney Godolphin, bearing the date 1643:

" From Francis Godolphin to John Rogers.

" For your coming over and making up your books, if it were not for displeasing somebody that I never will if I can helpe it, I should be very glad of seeing you, and the place is worth your seeing too; indeed I like it, much better than I did expect, though I must confess I came much the more willingly hither because I was not well at ease where I was . . . There has noe ship come in hither since Jack went, but a Falmouth warrier, which received a broadside from one of the Parl. ships the day before.

" I conceive there can be no possibility of peace. Our God be merciful to us . . . to come hither, considering how glad I am at all hours to have you by me, and the novelty of the place for a few days would entertain you contentedly enough, and more than a few would tire you ten times more than Compton did. There are also some things about this place, I doe not mean the fortification, but the grounds, wherein your judgment, having viewed it, would be of use to me.

" I would also that you should see my patience, for this place, in respect of an Absolute want of all welcome company is a strange change to me.

"Yet a very honest man, borne here, may live very happily, as many doe, that would not change for twice soe much a year in Cornwall. For all this, I would by noe means be guilty of drawing you hither if it in any way dislike your best friend. We have seen noe doubtful ship upon the coast a great while . . .

"I have received a warrant from the King to carry over two-hundred men more, for the safeguard of the fort at Scilly for the summer; the estates of divers delinquents, as the Lord

Star Castle, St. Mary's, built in 1593 to protect the islands from attack from possible further Spanish Armadas.

St. Mary's harbour from an old print, 1669, showing the old quay and Rat Island before the new quay was constructed.

D

The entrance to the Elizabethan fortress of Star Castle.

Robartes, both Trevills, Boscawen, Sergnt Aubin, and Erisey appointed to be sold . . . out of which £600 is, in the first place, to be paid to me, for provision of a magasin of victualles at Scilly."

This letter was written during the Civil War. In this struggle between Charles I and Parliament, Star Castle afforded a refuge for the Cavaliers. In 1646, when the Parliamentarians, under General Fairfax, had defeated the Royalist army at Bodmin, the Prince of Wales (afterwards Charles II), accompanied by Lord Colpepper and Sir Edward Hyde, left Pendennis Castle and sailed for the Scillies.

The Prince wished to keep his foot on British ground to the last, and sent Lord Colpepper, two days after he landed, to acquaint the Queen (in France) " with the wants and incommodities of the place ". Star Castle had been considered a position of great strength, but did not, in this respect, answer their expectations. Lords Capel and Hopton were unable, owing to contrary winds, to sail from St. Michael's Mount to join them for upwards of a month, but when they did they brought a " trumpet" from Fairfax, bearing a letter from Parliament, requesting the Prince to come and " reside in such a place and with such council and attendants as the Parliament should think fit ". The Prince refused and observed " that he had remained in Scilly because he wished to be among his people, but that as in six weeks he had not received more than one day's victual from the mainland, he should be compelled to depart ".

On the day after the arrival of the " trumpet," a Parliamentary fleet of twenty-seven ships encompassed the islands, but a heavy gale setting in on that rocky coast, in two hours the vessels all dispersed. In Lady Fanshawe's Memoirs there is an account of her adventures in connection with the Prince's expedition to Scilly:

" Five days after, the Prince and all his council embark themselves in a ship called the ' Phoenix ' for the Isles of Scilly. They went from the Land's End, and so did we; being accompanied with many gentlemen of that country, among whom was Sir Francis Basset, Governor of the Mount, an honest gentleman, and so were all his family, and in particular we receive great civility from them. But we left our house and furniture with Captain Bluett who promised to keep them until such a time as we could dispose of them, but when we sent he said he had been plundered of them, notwithstanding it was well known he lost nothing of his own. At that time this loss went deep with us, for we lost to the value of £200 and more, but, as the proverb says, ' an evil chance seldom comes alone ', we having put all our present estate into two trunks; and carried them aboard with us in a ship commanded by Sir Nicholas Crispe (whose skill and honesty the master and seamen had no opinion of) my husband was forced to appease a mutiny, which his miscarriage caused, and taking out money to pay the seamen, that night following they broke open one of our trunks and took out a bag of £60, and a quantity of gold lace with our best clothes and linen, with all my combs, gloves and ribbons, which amounted to £300 more. The next day, after being pillaged, and extremely sick and big with child, I was set on shore almost dead, in the Island of Scilly. When we had got to our quarters near the Castle where the Prince lay, I went immediately to bed, which was so vile that my footman ever lay in a better, and we but three in the whole house, which consisted of four rooms or rather, partitions, two low rooms and two little lofts with a ladder to go up; in one of these they kept dried fish, which was their trade, and in this my husband's two clerks lay. One there was for my sister, and one for myself, and one amongst the rest of the servants; but when I washed in the morning I was so cold, I knew not what to do, but the daylight discovered that my bed was near swimming in the sea, which the owner told us it never did so but at spring-tide. With this we were destitute of clothes; and meat and fuel for half the Court to serve them a month, was not to be had in the whole Island, and truly we begged our daily bread of God; for we thought every meal our last. The council sent for provisions to France, which served us, but they were bad and little of them; then after three weeks and odd days we set sail for the Isle of Jersey, where we safely arrived, praise be God, beyond the belief of all the beholders from that Island, for the pilot, not knowing the way into the harbour, sailed over the rocks, but being spring-tide, and by chance high water, God be praised, His Highness and all of us come safe ashore through so great a danger ".

The Prince had remained at Star Castle from 4th March to the 16th April, 1646.

From the summer of 1646 till the autumn of 1648 Scilly was in the hands of the Roundheads, but Sir John Grenville who had been appointed Governor held the islands for the following two and a half years for the Royalists till 1651, the Scillies being the last foothold of the Cavaliers in England, from whence they fitted out cruisers and harassed all Parliamentary shipping passing to or from the English, Irish and Bristol Channels. Strategically, the Scillies are well placed for this and the Scillonians themselves were naturally Royalist in sympathy, and had resented the Roundheads.

Parliament was very much alarmed by the Royalist strength in Scilly. The Calendar of State Papers of 1648 reports the proceedings of a Committee of both Houses of Parliament:

" To write to the Committee of Cornwall and the Governor of Plymouth and to Sir Hardress Waller, to take care to regain the Island of Scilly before it be further strengthened or the Castle victualed. To notify to Lord General (Fairfax) the revolt of Scilly . . . "

But while Sir John Grenville was doing his duty by his king, that monarch was reported to have endeavoured to pledge the Islands as security for a loan of £50,000 from merchants in Amsterdam.

Reinforcements came in 1649 when Prince Rupert brought a large number of soldiers from Ireland to aid the garrison, saying that he would make Scilly " a second Venice ".

Whitlock, in his Memorials, quotes the following:—

" Letters, 26 June 1649, mention that a Frigate of Sir John Granville, Governor of Scilly, with two Bras Guns, 24 Muskets and 24 Oars, coming near Swansea, the Governor of Cardiff sent out Boats, pursued the Frigate from Creek to Creek, and at length took her, and the men, except the Capt. and some few, who got ashore."

" Letters (6 March 1650) of several ships taken by Pyrates of Scilly and Jersey. Letters of 15 March of the want of Frigates on the Western Coast to keep in the Jersey and Scilly Pirates, and of their taking several Merchantmen, and none of the Parliament Frigates to help them. Letters of 19 March of the Pyracies committed by those of Jersey and Scilly."

Apparently the Royalists in Scilly were in such straits that they were forced to commandeer provisions from the ships of any nation passing near enough for the purpose, because, on the plea that Dutch shipping had been seized, Admiral Van Tromp appeared off the islands and demanded satisfaction. Van Tromp's real purpose, however, was to obtain possession of the islands, and for this purpose he first proposed to hold them for the King against the Parliament, and then offered compensation to Sir John Grenville for their surrender. But that faithful officer replied that it would be inconsistent with his duty to his country to abandon a post, the maintenance of which had been committed to him by his Sovereign. Unable to persuade Sir John to hand over English land to a foreigner, even though Sir John was at war with his own country-men, Van Tromp sailed away and announced at Plymouth that he had declared war with the Isles of Scilly and was ready to proceed with Parliament against them.

The possibility that privations might eventually outweigh Grenville's patriotism and result in the Scillies' becoming a Dutch base, together with the clamours of the Parliamentary representatives of the merchant interests whose ships and cargoes were being plundered by the Royalist " pirates " of Scilly, at length determined the government to send an expeditionary force to subdue the islands.

The parliamentary fleet which set sail from Plymouth in April, 1651, was fitted out under the direction and command of the veteran parliamentary commanders General Blake and Sir George Ascue (Ayscue).

The itinerary of the expedition is as follows according to letters quoted in Whitlock's " Memorials ":

" 17 April 1651: Letters: ' That Lieutenant-Colonel Clarke with nine companies of foot, set sail from Plymouth for Scilly Islands.'

17 April, 1651: Letters: ' That Van Tromp came to Pendennis and related that he had been to Scilly to demand reparation for the Dutch ship and goods taken by them; and receiving no satisfactory answer, he had, according to his Commission, declared war on them.'

21 April: ' That Van Tromp lay before Scilly and declared that he would assist the English against it'.

24 April: Letters: ' Of the Fleet's arrival at Scilly and of the guns heard from thence.'

26 April: Letters: ' That 2,000 of the Parliament's soldiers and
seamen were landed in the little Isles on the West of Scilly, and
that the Ordnance were heard thundering there many hours
together.'

2 May: Letters: ' That the Parliament's Fleet at Scilly had taken
New Grimsby after 3 times being beaten off, and that they had
taken 2 Irish Frigates, one of 30 and the other of 24 guns.'

3rd May: ' That the Parliamentary soldiers had taken all the
Islands except St. Mary's and had taken 3 of their Frigates,
killed 14 of their men, and taken 120 prisoners. That of the
Parliamentary Forces, 8 were killed and 20 wounded; that they
intended to send a summons to St. Mary's Island, and if they
refused, then to attempt it.'

8 May: ' That General Blake and Sir George Ascue with the
Fleet at Scilly intend to fall upon St. Mary's Island, that the
Governor thereof, Sir John Grenville, sent to them for a Treaty,
which was agreed, but took no effect, and thereupon the great
guns played upon St. Mary's.'

12 May: ' Letters from Sir George Ascue of the action at
Scilly, that Captain Morris behaved himself most gallantly in
the storming of the Island. That the Scilly Islands are a key that
opens a passage to several Nations.'

30 May: ' That the Foot of Scilly entered at St. Mary's Island,
and that those in the Castle were in great want of water.'[1]"

The following account is related by Jos. Lereck in a seventeenth
century document, and quoted by " Lanje ":

" We of the Parliament Forces, had laid at sea from Saturday,
April 12th, till Thursday, the 17th, when in the morning . . . we
put our soldiers in boats to endeavour to make a landing on
Tresco; one party was to land in a sandy bay near the Fort at
Old Grimsby Harbour, and the other in a more stony bay,
somewhat to the westward. We had not reckoned on the
strength of the tide, which was on the ebb, and some of our
boats were grounded on the rocks and others carried out of
their course. So orders were given for all the boats to make
straight for Old Grimsby Harbour and we sheltered by a rock
in the Channel until we could make a joint attack. We then

---

1 There is some difficulty in reconciling the dates in the various accounts.

moved forward, but the pilots and many of the rowers had been taken up in the West Country and were very backward in the service, misguided us, and we came to a little island called Norwithiel, standing in the entrance to the Harbour, and within half-a-musket shot of Tresco. The Pilots swore that it was Trescoe, but Captain Bowden was doubtful of it, as none of the enemy came to oppose our landing. Some of the Companies had landed and the boats were aground, but in order that the opportunity might not be lost, the rest of the boats were ordered forward. They were again misguided, and came to a rocky part of Tresco where it was difficult to land. The enemy brought down a body of musketeers, and there was hot firing on our boats from behind rocks on the shore. Our boats were at a disadvantage, being so thickly crammed with men that they could not use their muskets. Here, we endured about 70 great shot beside musketry in abundance, so that many of the boats turned helm and rowed out of range, notwithstanding the struggle of Col. Clarke and other officers. After half-an-hour we all withdrew to Norwithiel, and found that our loss was not so great as was feared. We then rowed to an adjacent Island called Teän, leaving three companies on Norwithiel. We spent a very cold and comfortless night on Teän, and the next day the enemy began firing great shot at us, which fell among our tents but did no great harm. We managed to get some much needed provisions ashore from the ships which were riding at a distance, and we prepared ourselves for a second attempt.

" We sent to Admiral Blake for a better supply of rowers for the boats, and he moreover sent about 200 seamen to attempt the assault with us. We resolved to storm the Enemy by night, and during the day we took careful observations of the Channel and the place of intended landing.

" We drew off our men from Norwithiel in the evening, with the exception of 80 men left to amuse the enemy while we attacked, and about 11 o'clock we set forward. By the mercy of God it was very calm, so that the enemy's frigates could not come up the Channel to do us any harm, although they fired some great shot at us.

" We made fires on Teän to deceive the enemy, and the smoke blew towards Tresco, which somewhat obscured our passage.

Yet the enemy discovered us when we were about half way over and fired much ordnance at us, with little hurt.

" The boats came up well together, and though at first forced back, we charged them so resolutely, even with clubbed muskets, that we worsted them, killed 1 captain, 14 men, took prisoners 4 captains and 167 men, the rest fleeing, and none had escaped had we been better acquainted with the Island. We had been opposed by 1,300 men—a greater strength by far than we had imagined.

" Let the exceeding goodness of God to this unthankful nation, in lopping off the bough, even with terror, and giving into our hands a place stuffed with men, a greater number by many than we were, and but yesterday a curse to our Maritime Affairs, a scourge to the Merchants, though invincible for strength, and desperate to attempt with so little loss in so short a time."

The sympathies of the inhabitants can be judged by the feat of the pilot called Nance, who, although " the most knowing pilot of the place ", led them to Norwithiel (Northwethel) affirming on his life it was Tresco.

When the Parliamentarians had conquered Tresco, General Blake erected an advance battery to command Broad and Crow Sounds. This battery could reach any ship that went into, or came out from, St. Mary's Harbour.

Sir John Grenville soon found his position untenable, since not only were his ships prevented from approaching the islands, but he was lamentably short of provisions of all kinds. It was not, however, until he had sought and obtained permission from his King, then in Holland, that Sir John Grenville consented to surrender on conditions[1]. It is possible that the conditions were exceptionally favourable on account of Sir John's known refusal to treat with Van Tromp, the potential enemy of their common country. The surrendering garrison was permitted to march out, together with

---

[1]   The document of surrender was headed as follows:—"Articles agreed on this xxiii day of May 1651, by and betweene Admirall Blake and Colonell Clerke, Commanders in chiefe of all the fforces by Sea or Land, in and about the Islands of Triscoe and Briar, of the one part, Sr. John Grenville, Knight, Governor of the Islands of St. Marye's and Agnes, in Scilly, on the behalfe of his Matie., on the other pt., touching the rendition of the sd. Isles of St. Marye's and Agnes, together with all the Castles, forts, fortresses, sconces and fortifications unto them belonging, to the use and behoof of the Parliam. of England as followeth . . ."

arms and horses, to the beat of drums and sound of trumpets, colours displayed and " matches lighted at both ends "—the last of the Cavaliers. They were about 1,500 men, with " enough commissioned officers to head an army ". It is not known at what point Van Tromp and his twelve ships left the scene.[1]

The men were transported to Ireland, Scotland and France, to which countries they probably belonged, while the Governor and some of the chief officers were taken to Plymouth, where Sir John Grenville was soon set at liberty and permitted to embark for the Continent to share the fortunes of his Royal Master, who later, created him Earl of Bath. " He attended the King in his greatest distresses, throughout all his disconsolate travels, in France, Flanders, Holland and the Isle of Jersey." There is a Cornish saying to the effect that " a Godolphin never wanted wit nor a Grenville loyalty ". One of the special provisions of the Treaty was that none of the islanders should suffer, and many Royalist gentlemen, including a representative of the Godolphin family, remained in Scilly to await better times.

Soon after this reduction of the islands in 1651, a strong circular tower, Oliver Cromwell's Castle, was built to command the Channel between New Grimsby and Bryher, and was manned by twenty men.[2] A garrison of six hundred was at the same time maintained in the islands but, not long after the surrender, Scilly appears to have been neglected, for we find a petition dated May 14th, 1658, from Lt.-Col. Joseph Hunkin, Governor of Scilly, to the Protector: " The stores of ammunition in the garrison are decayed; there are only 77 barrels of powder left here

---

[1] It is stated in " Cornwall in the Great Civil War " by Miss Mary Coates, that the Islands of Scilly were surrendered to the combined English and Dutch fleets. The Victoria County History on the other hand, states that Van Tromp appeared off the islands in March, 1651, with a fleet, demanding reparation for piracies committed on Dutch vessels. The Council of State at once took alarm and made representations to The Hague that Tromp's presence was an unfriendly act and Blake was ordered to take command of Sir George Ayscue's fleet, then ready to sail for the West Indies, fight Tromp if necessary, and not to leave Cornish waters until he had reduced the Isles of Scilly.

[2] The date of Cromwell's Castle has been disputed. It has been suggested (see p.233 *The Scillonian* Vol. XXXII, No. 132 of December 1957) that the " castle dates from the reign of Edward V and was probably being erected in 1550." If this is so then two points must be answered: (i) A seaman's map of about 1585 in the British Museum by Captain John Davis shows King Charles's Castle but not Cromwell's Castle. (ii) In 1600 Godolphin wished to fortify Hangman's Island because the guns of King Charles' Castle were sited too high to be brought to bear on the Sound. This would not have been necessary if Cromwell's Castle had been in existence at that time.

by the enemy at the surrender of the islands, which is now unfit for service. There is also a great want of Saker and minion shot, there being only two shots apiece for all these guns on the islands. Begs 200 barrels of powder and three tons of shot so that he may be able to defend the Islands in case of any vicissitude of affairs."

For a time, Star Castle provided a very convenient place for political and other prisoners. Dr. John Bastwick was the first prisoner of note known to have been confined in Star Castle. He was a persistent pamphleteer and critic of Archbishop Laud in the reign of King Charles I. His most outspoken pamphlet concluded with the words . . . " From plague, pestilence and famine, from bishops, priests and deacons, good Lord deliver us." He was sentenced by the Star Chamber in 1637 to a fine of £5,000, to be deprived of his ears,[1] to suffer in the pillory, and then to be confined in the Isles of Scilly. He was released in 1640 after three years' imprisonment in the islands, but died soon afterwards.

Another prisoner was the Duke of Hamilton who, in 1643, was consigned to the care of Sir Francis Godolphin at Star Castle, with particular instructions from the King as to his custody. In 1655, Oliver Cromwell awarded a pension of 10/- a week to John Biddle, the celebrated Socinian (Unitarian), and sent him to the Isles of Scilly for confinement to keep him " out of the way of his persecutors."

At the restoration in 1660, King Charles II, who had himself spent six weeks at Star Castle in 1646 after fleeing from Fairfax's victorious army, sent three prominent Roundheads to be imprisoned in the Isles of Scilly. Sir John Wildman, the Anabaptist and political malcontent, described in Pepys' Diary as " a false fellow to everybody", was six years a prisoner, first in the Tower of London, then in Star Castle, and later in Pendennis Castle. Macauley says, " With Wildman's fanaticism was joined a tender care for his own safety, grazing the edge of treason." He died in 1693.

Sir John Ireton, a zealous republican and brother of the famous regicide, was Lord Mayor of London in 1658. He was imprisoned in Star Castle in 1662, released later, and imprisoned again in 1685, dying in 1689.

---

[1] Dr. Bastwick's wife stood on a stool, kissed him, placed the ears in a clean handkerchief, and then took them away with her.

Another Puritan prisoner was Sir Harry Vane, one of the most influential statesman of the Commonwealth, described as a man of a noble and generous mind. He was kept a prisoner in the Isles of Scilly for two years and, although King Charles II had promised that his life should be spared, he had powerful enemies at Court and was beheaded on Tower Hill in 1662. Mr. Pepys was told by Will Swan that " Sir H. Vane died as much a martyr and saint as ever a man did and that the King hath lost more by that man's death than he can get again in a good while."

One further reference to Star Castle as a place of confinement is on record when in 1681 we find that " seven popish priests " were conveyed thither from Newgate.

A visitor of note in the seventeenth century was the Grand Duke Cosmo III, in 1669, who left on record in his diary an interesting account of his stay, together with a view of Star Castle as it then existed. He speaks in terms of praise of the islands and of his reception, and mentions that the castle and adjacent batteries were armed with " 130 very beautiful iron culverins " with a garrison of 200 men at a cost to the King of about £4,000 per annum.

The fortifications were allowed to fall into decay, but, in the war with Spain in 1740 they were again put into a state of defence and many new batteries were erected on " The Hugh ". The strong entrance gateway and the bastions around the Hugh itself were erected at this period. The gateway bears the date 1742. In this year the following instructions were issued by the Governor from London where he resided:

Orders—by the Rt. Hon. Francis Earl of Godolphin, Governor and Proprietor of His Majesty's Islands of Scilly.

ORDERS TO BE OBSERVED AND OBEYED BY THE GARRISON AND ISLANDERS.

(1)   That in the absence of the Governor and Lt. Governor, the said garrison and islanders do obey the Commanding Officer for the time being, as their Magistrate.

(2)   That the islanders on firing of the warning gun do forthwith repair to his Majesty's Star Castle for the defence of the said islands.

(3)   That the master gunner and gunners do not presume to go off St. Mary's island without leave from the Commanding Officer for the time being.

(4)   That no islander presume to go to the main, without leave from the Commanding Officer for the time being, especially in time of war.

(5)   That all pilots make a report immediately to the Commanding Officer for the time being, of all ships they pilot in, with their force, and number of men, and that no pilot presume to carry any ship out without first seeking its clearance from his Majesty's Star Castle.

(6)   That all persons who land in any of the said islands be forthwith brought before the Commanding Officer for the time being to be examined by him.

(7)   That these orders be published in the said islands, and hung up in his Majesty's Star Castle there.

GODOLPHIN.

St. James', 29th May, 1742.

The following is a list of the Governors of the Isles of Scilly bearing Commissions:

Hon. Sir Francis Godolphin	1593
Hon. Sir William Godolphin	?
Hon. Francis Godolphin	1640
Hon. Sir John Grenville (afterwards Earl of Bath)	1651
Lt.-Col. Joseph Hunkin	1658
Hon. Sidney Godolphin	1702
Major Bennett	?
Rt. Hon. Francis Earl of Godolphin	1733

Gradually the military establishment in Scilly was reduced. In 1822 it consisted of a Lieutenant-Governor, a master gunner, four gunners and two or three aged sergeants; in 1857, five invalids (His Majesty's Company of Invalids) manned the fortifications; and, finally, in 1863, it was left to the care of one elderly caretaker. In the eighteenth century the salary of the Governor of the Isles of Scilly was £1,821 10s.

The last military Governors were Lt.-Col. Geo. Vigoureux (immortalised by Sir Arthur Quiller-Couch in his story " Major

Vigoureux ") and Major-General J. N. Smyth, who died in Scilly in 1838.

Within recent times the Government has considered making a naval base of Scilly, and new batteries were constructed at a cost of a quarter of a million pounds as late as 1905. The guns were hoisted laboriously up Garrison Hill and mounted in the forts. They fired practice rounds aiming for a target at a wooden post mounted on the " Cow " off St. Agnes.

In the 1st World War a naval and seaplane base was established in Scilly with concrete ramps at Porthmellon, St. Mary's, and near New Grimsby, Tresco, with about a thousand men stationed in the islands. In the 2nd World War the islands served as an air and sea base in the Battle of the Atlantic.

VI

THE SCILLONIANS AND ROBERT MAYBEE

THERE IS LITTLE WRITTEN EVIDENCE OF THE LIVES OF the inhabitants of Scilly before the 16th century and even in Domesday Book (1086) Scilly is not mentioned. But there is good archaeological evidence that the islands were inhabited by people of the Early Bronze Age. At Bants Carn, St. Mary's, and on Par Beach, St. Martin's, and also at St. Agnes, the bases of round stone huts have been disclosed; and from the surrounding middens (refuse dumps), fragments of pottery have been found similar to those found in barrows, and these help to date the inhabitants. In the middens, bones of horses, of sheep, and of a small breed of deer, together with stone and bone tools, stone querns for grinding corn, and innumerable shells of limpets (one of the staple articles of diet on the sea coast in those days) have been unearthed. Flint scrapers for dressing skins of animals, awls, whorls and spindles for weaving garments, stone mace-heads and flint arrowheads have been collected in quantity.

The earliest invaders of the south-west of Britain seem to have been the Iberians, short dark-haired people, traces of whose stock are said to survive today in isolated parts of Cornwall and in Scilly. From the sixth century onwards successive waves of tall, fair-haired, blue-eyed Celts penetrated to Cornwall with their religion of Druidism, but the evidence for Druidism in Scilly is very uncertain. The antiquarian Dr. Borlase professed to find innumerable sacrificial stones in Scilly, but the natural weathering of stone by the elements is so bizarre that human agency must be doubted. But Troutbeck supports Borlase in attributing rock basins on Scilly to the sacrificial rites of Druidism; Gilbert calls them " supposed relics "; North considers them the work of chance; and Whitfield on the same subject reminds us of a story: "Here," quoth Monkbarns, waxing eloquent as he described to a guest the imaginary Roman camp, "here was the Praetorian Gate." " Praetorian here, Praetorian there," replied Edie Ochiltee, " I mind well the diggin o't it! " It is now generally accepted that the rock basins, including those fine examples on Peninnis Head, are entirely the work of nature unaided by man.

The economic prosperity of the islanders has fluctuated greatly. Today, they are relatively prosperous and the Isles of Scilly fully deserve their name of " Fortunate Islands ". But in past centuries the islanders have suffered greatly, and for the most part may be said to have scratched a living only with the greatest difficulty and in the face of enormous dangers. Coastal regions were particularly susceptible to attack and, in Scilly, the elements alone were sufficient to make life hazardous.

After 2500 B.C. and until about 1400 B.C., Scilly and Cornwall seem to have been in contact with traders from Brittany and from the Mediterranean, particularly the Phoenicians, seeking tin. Scilly may also have served as a port of call for the gold trade between Ireland, Spain and the Mediterranean. In the Middle Bronze Age (about 1400 to 1000 B.C.), however, this trade began to take an overland course (according to Hencken) through England across the English Channel to Europe, and then overland to the head of the Adriatic. Consequently, South-West England suffered an economic decline due to the contraction of the sea traffic. But in the later Bronze Age, between 1000 B.C. and 350 B.C. there was some revival of this sea trade, and tin mining flourished in this period as never before, though the beginnings may go back as early as 2000 B.C. Tin became the main source of trading income and the area was relatively well populated. The discovery of tin in other places, notably Spain, at the beginning of the Christian era, caused some decline in the tin trade, but it revived again in the Middle Ages and continued in Cornwall until 1918, by then being considered no longer economically worthwhile to work on a large scale, though an occasional mine is still worked.

In the 5th century A.D. the Damnonii spread over most of South-West Britain and possibly Scilly and colonised Armorica (Brittany). This link between Cornwall and Brittany has long since disappeared; but, even today as an Englishman is something of a foreigner to a Cornishman so is a Frenchman, to a Breton.

Strabo describes the inhabitants of Scilly as wearing a dress similar to that of the people of the south of Spain, a black mantle sagum or loena. The descendants of the Iberians and Celts undoubtedly mixed with the successive waves of West Britons, Saxons, Northmen and emigrants from Scotland, Ireland, Gaul and the Mediterranean, the geographical situation of the islands making it inevitable that a great variety of people sojourned there, some of whom may have remained.

Eustathius calls the natives of Scilly " Melancholi " because of their habit of wearing black clothing down to their ankles; Solinus says that " they lived according to the old manner; they had no markets, nor did money pass among them; but they gave in exchange one thing for another, and so provided themselves with necessaries; they were very religious, both men and women, and pretended to have great skill in the Art of Divination, or in foretelling of what was to come. And as to the healthful state of their climate, Sardus was persuaded that they lived so long till they were weary of life; because they threw themselves from a Rock into the Sea, in hopes of a better life."

Camden states, of his time (1586), that: " The inhabitants are all newcomers[1], but remains show much previous habitation." This presents a mystery connected with the islands. One may speculate exhaustively as to the reason why a total population should have deserted the islands and then be replaced with newcomers. It may, of course, have been due to some convulsion of nature, such as an inundation of land that would cause a widespread sense of insecurity and consequent emigration; it may have been due to some pestilence or to a raid that might have annihilated them; or perhaps merely to hard living and the prospect of better subsistence elsewhere. Historical records do not help us, but no Scillonian today would claim descent from inhabitants of the islands before the 16th century. It is probable that the earliest settlers that provide a connecting link with present day families were squatters. Some are known to have come from Scotland and Ireland, and no doubt Cornwall contributed its share. Many of the existing families of Scillonians, or of Scillonians who were until recently resident in the isles, trace their descent from the Godolphins. The Edwards, Crudges, MacFarlands, Mumfords, Banfields, and Tregarthens are all connected with the Godolphin family through the marriage of Ursula, a daughter of Sir Francis Godolphin, to John Crudge, of Scilly. But it was probably the popularity of the early Godolphins that resulted in a number of families leaving Cornwall for the Scillies, and it is likely that this influx of

---

[1] Settlers introduced by early Godolphins in or after the reign of Edward VI (1547 – 1553)

highly favoured mainlanders completely dominated the previous inhabitants, who, at that period, must have lived at a very low subsistence level. An example of this is the story of an inhabitant of Bryher, employed on the construction of the fortifications on " The Hugh ", St. Mary's, who rowed himself daily backwards and forwards across the two miles or so of sea and received, for his no doubt long and arduous labours, the princely sum of 6d. a week.

Since at various times a large garrison of soldiers has been kept on the islands, including Grenadier Guards and a company of the Bedford Regiment—which, tradition has it, was forgotten and left on the islands—it is certain that a good deal of inter-marriage resulted, and no doubt many time-expired men, whose wives had relations on the isles, settled there. In 1669, Duke Cosmo III reports on his visit to the Isles: " Corn of late began to be scarce, in consequence of the increase of the population produced by marriages of the soldiers of the garrison with the islanders, but this has been remedied for some years past by forbidding them to marry."

Each island has a generic nickname, which is still occasionally in use, but rapidly dying out. St. Mary's men are Bulldogs. Tresco men are Caterpillars (probably associated with smuggling, and files of keg-carriers as seen in the moonlight).

Bryher men are Thorns, or " lop-sided " or " one-sided ". It is frequently averred that whatever is done by the men of Bryher is aslant, that they walk askew, carry their heads slightly bent sideways, hold a cup or glass at an angle, and generally appear " one-sided ".

St. Martin's men are Ginnicks (etymology unknown) and at one time were remarkable for the number of them with red or sandy hair. They are said to be the most independent of all the different island populations. The island is supposed to have been peopled from Sennen in Cornwall. They are hard workers and their womenfolk often have high shrill voices which it used to be claimed could sometimes carry to St. Mary's. North says that in his day St. Martin's people tended to be tall and thin.

St. Agnes folk are called Turks and are popularly supposed to be short and thickset, with dark hair and eyes, partly the result it has been alleged of inter-marriage with stranded sailors from the wreck of a Spanish ship. " Their speech is short and crisp, and they grow long silken beards." In the 19th century the menfolk of

Preparing the graves for the victims of the S.S. Schiller, 1875, with Old Town Church in the background. 311 persons were drowned when the transatlantic liner (in her day one of the largest ships afloat) was wrecked on the Western Rocks in fog.

The Bishop Rock Lighthouse.
" Beautiful, dark and solitary,
The first of England that spoke to me."
Laurence Binyon

St. Agnes, even more so than in the other islands, specialised in putting out quickly in their gigs to supply pilots to passing ships. More recently, St. Agnes people have shown a remarkable spirit of co-operation in the construction of a six-foot wide concrete surface on the road stretching across the back of the island.

Tresco people, according to North, are of intermediate stature between those of St. Martin's and St. Agnes. St. Mary's people are more cosmopolitan and have no peculiarities of their own. Their main family surnames used to alternate between Banfields, Edwardes, Tregarthens, Bluets, Gibsons and Mumfords. Certain surnames still predominate on the off-islands, but this is less noticeable nowadays: St. Agnes has several families named Hicks and Legge; Tresco, Bryher and St. Martin's have Jenkins, Pender, Ashford and Ellis.

But for over a century there has been constant and daily intercourse between the islands so that the young men have had no difficulty in finding wives from islands other than their own, and this has so weakened the especial characteristics of the populations of the individual islands that the differences are now hardly perceptible. It is said, however, that the social climate on each island still varies greatly, and that the inhabitants of certain islands are co-operative and friendly while on others they are less so. These generalisations are transient, however, and are most likely due to the qualities of individuals who make up the island communities at any given time, rather than to any particular facet of the social climate inherent in the community.

In the early days, from the time of Athelstan onwards, the Scillonians must have been industrious, tilling the soil by battling with the special enemies of agriculture on Scilly—the strong winds and burning salt spray. Yet none of this would appear to have been worth a comment by those who have left us fragmentary records, although the punishment of wrongdoers was " news " and thus has received a quite unfair measure of publicity. The Crown leases conferred on the lessees conclusive jurisdiction in all plaints and causes—heresies, treasons, matters of life and limb and Admiralty questions excepted. Until the reign of George IV (1827) the clerical order had benefit of clergy (as on the mainland) and were exempt from civil punishment.

The lessee, who was termed the Lord Proprietor, created a " Court of Twelve " to administer local affairs, and this court, by virtue of its isolation and situation, and the absence of the lessee, soon assumed dictatorial powers. At one time we find them issuing an order prohibiting masters of vessels from importing strangers, or exporting residents, under a penalty of £10. At another time a troublesome thief is ordered to be put on board the first of his Majesty's ships of war that might call, women were ducked at the quay head, and men and women were ordered to be publicly whipped. Paupers were deported to the mainland. Towards the end of the eighteenth century a man on St. Agnes was charged with Sabbath-breaking by digging potatoes, but owing to his extreme poverty the case was dismissed on the delinquent promising " not to do it again ". At about the same period there is record of a woman on St. Mary's who was sentenced to receive 50 lashes on the bare back for stealing a cotton shirt. But since England possessed the harshest penal code of any European country in the 18th century, and stealing five shillings or more from a shop was among several hundred other crimes punishable by death, such severe sentences must not be taken as peculiar to Scilly.

Borlase says, however, that in his time (1756), the Court of Twelve " meet once a month, hear complaints, and compose some little disputes, but rather by compromise than decision, and this is all the government they have, without calling in the Military Power ... common immoralities escape all reprehension ... so that the people are left too much to their own will and as the Islands have but the Shadow of Government the good feel not the benefit of it because 'tis but a shadow, nor the wicked the weight of it for the same reason."

Heath, an officer of the Garrison, who wrote in 1750, and must have been a wit, says: " The spiritual court of Scilly is the ' ducking chair ' at the quay head, into which offenders in language or morality are put by order of the ' Court of Twelve ', and receive their purification in salt or holy water. The punishments in Scilly are fines, whipping or ducking. There is no prison for the confinement of offenders, which shows that the people are upright enough not to require any, or that the place is a confinement in itself. No venomous insects or reptiles or attorneys or sheriff's officers are ever harboured in these islands."

He enumerates the trades exercised in Hugh Town in his time: bakers, brewers, coopers, butchers, weavers, tailors, mantua-makers, shoe-makers, sail-makers, joiners, carpenters, masons, smiths and periwig-makers. Islanders, by the nature of their situation, develop an ability to master all trades, and it is not surprising that the Scillonians have weathered many economic "blizzards" by the simple process of changing their means of livelihood.

In 1684, the making of kelp, an alkali of value to glassmakers, soap-makers and bleachers, was commenced, and immense quantities of seaweed were collected and burnt in kilns. This industry continued for some hundred and fifty years and became one of the mainstays of the economic life. There was also a certain amount of weaving and long-line fishing for ling, a good deal of which was dried, salted and exported. Scilly ling was famous. Lord Nelson wrote from Toulon to a friend in Plymouth, in October, 1803, thanking him for a present of Scilly ling, which he had "much enjoyed".

During and after the Napoleonic Wars (1805–1814) there was widespread distress in the islands and particularly on the off-islands. The findings of a deputation sent by the Penzance magistrates in 1819 give a good illustration of the troubles of previous years. The causes of distress in the off-islands, according to the report, were as follows:

" (1) To the bad harvests of the two preceding years.
" (2) To the failure during the preceding year of the means of making kelp.
" (3) To the decrease of employment in piloting resulting from the establishment of branch pilots, by which employment was monopolised by very few hands.
" (4) To the failure in a considerable degree of the ling fishery.
" (5) To the entire suppression of smuggling by the Preventive boat system, by the loss of which contraband trade the Islanders lost their chief means of support."

The fifth point is interesting as indicating the extent of smuggling on the islands during the 18th century. The activity became not only the life-blood of Scilly's economy but also a way of life for the inhabitants. The customs officers who attempted to combat it were not helped by the requirement that in any prosecution the officer making the charge had to pay the expense. This meant that normally only clear-cut cases were brought to book and, considering the amount of contraband, very little was, in fact, seized. Probably the off-islands were the most favourable points for operating the traffic, and many a small boat ostensibly carrying a pilot may well also have been running contraband. An East Indiaman bound up Channel may well have parted with some of her cargo of muslins and silks to be hidden away perhaps in an off-island cave. Spirits, brandy, rum, wines, and tobacco would probably constitute the greater part of smuggled goods as was the case around other parts of England's coast because of the relatively high duties on these commodities. After 1784, the stationing of a protection vessel in Scilly probably made smuggling more difficult. In 1790, an Act of Parliament allowed the legal costs of cases of smuggling to be met by the Commissioners out of the sale of seizures. An inducement to greater efficiency was given to revenue officers by allowing them to keep a small share of the proceeds. After this smuggling gradually declined till it's virtual suppression became a source of economic depression in the islands.

In consequence of the grim report of 1819 which bears witness to this distress, and it's publication in *The Times* and other London newspapers, a General Committee was formed and subscriptions invited. No less than £9,000 was collected, a sum that was administered by a Resident Agent for the Committee, and used mainly in an attempt to establish a pilchard and mackerel fishery by means of the purchase of suitable boats, the repair of the existing ones and the erection of storehouses.

Unfortunately, either owing to misdirection of this enterprise, or maladministration, or possibly to the vagaries of the pilchard (which is somewhat unreliable in its habits), the expected alleviation of conditions did not take place, and the distress continued for some years. Or, as the proverb has it:

" Scads and taties all the week
And conger-pies on Sundays."

The island of Samson, which supported at one time some forty or fifty inhabitants, was finally evacuated in 1855 owing to the poorness of the living and the difficulty of administering the older people there. Nineteen men and boys from Samson lost their lives in the shipwreck of a French barque that had been captured during the Napoleonic Wars, and which struck on the Wolf Rock when they were taking her as a prize to Devonport, and the island never recovered from this disaster.

A close observer of Scilly and the Scillonians was Robert Maybee. He was a ballad singer and poet who was born on St. Mary's in 1810, and died there in 1884. In his later years he was reduced to hawking fruit and doing odd jobs about the islands, but his songs have always been treasured by Scillonians. His native charm and simplicity of character shine through the records he has left, and the history of the islands has been enriched by his artless but no doubt accurate descriptions of the life around him in the nineteenth century. He was an insignificant-looking little man with weak blue eyes and curly hair, and he could neither read nor write.

The following is one of Robert Maybee's word pictures describing the wreck of the "Association", the "Eagle" and the "Romney" in 1701, when Sir Cloudesley Shovel, so the story goes, refused to take the advice of one of his crew, a Scillonian, and ran his ship on the rocks with the loss of two thousand men.

" Dark on the Gilston's rocky shore
    The mist came lowering down,
And night with all her deepening gloom
    Put on her sable crown.

From sea a wailing sound is heard,
    And the seamew's shrilly cry,
And booming surge and shrieking birds
    Proclaim strange danger nigh.

Wrong you steer, Sir Cloudesley, sure;
    The rocks of Scilly shun;
Northern move, or no sailor here
    Will see to-morrow's sun.

Hold, wretch! Dare tell your Admiral
    What dangers to evade?
I'll hang you up on yon yard-arm
    Before your prayers are said.

Oh, Admiral, before I die
    Let someone read aloud
The one hundred and ninth dread Psalm
    To all this sailor crowd.

Let it be done, cursed mutineer;
    As if I know not how
To steer my Association clear
    Of every danger now.

The Psalm was read, the wretch was hung;
    Drear darkness stalked around;
Whilst aloft the dead man swung,
    Three ships had struck the ground.

How sad and awful was the sight,
    How black and dark the shore.
Two thousand souls went down that night,
    And ne'er saw daylight more.

One man alone of that brave crew
    Was saved to tell the tale.
How swift and sure God's vengeance came;
    He can alone prevail."

EXTRACTS FROM
" SIXTY-EIGHT YEARS' EXPERIENCE
ON THE SCILLY ISLANDS "

By Robert Maybee

" When I was young I many times wished I had been a scholar, that I might have written a long history of the Scilly Islands; but, being no scholar and in fact, unable to read or write, it was useless my thinking of making a book, so I gave up all idea of it until the year 1883. I was working in Tresco at that time, and in the evenings, when I had leisure, walking around the hills and thinking of what had passed on the islands in my lifetime, I found that I could remember everything that had happened in the islands for 68 years just as if it had occurred on that day. It then came into my mind that I would have a little book written if I could get someone to write it for me as I told it to him, about changes in life and trade and ship-wrecks and loss of life and also some pieces of poetry of my own composition . . .

" I asked the master of the house at which I lodged whether he would write a little book for me in the winter evenings, and he was agreeable. The first line of this book was put to paper on 5th November, 1883, my age at that time being 74 years. I chose that day to begin my book because 50 or 60 years ago it used to be a great holiday on this island, being known as "Ringing Tide", when all the boys were looking forward to having a day's holiday to ring the church bell.

"At that time Scilly was a fine place for catching fish. There were more than four times as many men on St. Mary's as there are now, and they were bigger and a much stronger race of people than the present inhabitants. They did not call themselves fishermen because a living could not be made out of fishing in those days; fish would not sell, as every man on the island could get as much as he liked to go after. It made no difference what their employment was—after they left work those who had no boats to go in could go out on the rocks and catch as many fish as they could carry home every night through the summer. Fifty years ago there were 23 public houses on St. Mary's and companies in all of them every evening; at this time there are only five and you will scarce see a man belonging to the island in any one of them— that is one great change that has taken place.

" I was born on 1st April, 1810, on the Head of the Peninnis, at St. Mary's, one of the Scilly Islands in the County of Cornwall, and that was my home till I was 42 years of age. My father was a native of the Isle of Wight, in the County of Hampshire, and came to the Scilly Islands to work the windmill that now stands on the Head of Peninnis. After the machinery was all taken out of the mill, it was fitted out for a signal station and now goes by the name of Rowel's Tower. My father had a house built about 60 yards to the east of the tower, and there he resided until the year 1834, when he died. Peninnis at that time was considered one of the pleasantest places on the island by visitors; it was a large open downs with no hedge on the west side of it till you got half-way to Buzza's Hill, and it was covered with long heath and wild flowers of various kinds which made it very pleasant in the summer time. It was about three-quarters of a mile from Hugh Town, with a footpath to it from Porth Cressa close by the seashore.

" The weather was different in those days to what it is now. The summers were very hot and we sometimes had calm weather for three or four weeks at a time, with a great number of small fishing boats all along the coast fishing, which made it very pleasant for travellers; and in winter time, with an easterly wind, there was a great number of ships coming in through the Sound every day, and a great many people used to go out to see them come round Peninnis Head. On the east side of Peninnis was Old Town Bay: a large pilot boat, two six-oared gigs and eight smaller boats belonging to Old Town were kept there, which could be manned at any time at a quarter-hour's notice, so that there was something new every day. I can remember everything that has happened on the islands since I was 5 years of age. The great battle of Waterloo was fought on the 18th June, 1815, and shortly after that, peace was proclaimed and a public dinner was held at St. Mary's in the open air and the town lit up well that night. I can remember being there with my father and mother: there were big guns mounted all round the Garrison which used to be fired on certain days in the year, such as the Queen's birthday. There were 100 soldiers in the Garrison, who used to march to church every Sunday and play the drum and fife as they marched: and a large number of men-of-war coming and going every day. The captains and officers and their boat crews would be ashore walking up and down the street, so you see there was more life in Scilly 68 years ago than there is now.

"After the French War was over, the 20 or 30 invalids who had been doing garrison duty were pensioned off with a small sum of money and they all stopped on the island till they died. Peninnis at that time was one of the best places for catching fish from the rocks. The pensioners, not having much work to do, often came out to catch fish mornings and evenings—some for pleasure and some for pastime: and after that most of the ladies and gentlemen in the town used to come out for pleasure. I have known as many as 40 or 50 people to be on the different rocks fishing on a fine summer's evening, and that was carried on for many years. In those days people could catch as much fish as they wished to have by going to the rocks to get them. When I was about 8 or 9 years old I could go down to the rocks at any time of the day and catch more small whiting fish than two men can get at this time by sailing all round the islands in a boat—unless it is at a time when the fish are in. There are 11 rocks around Peninnis where we used to go fishing. I shall name them. Beginning at the west side of

Peninnis, there is Carn Michael, The Chair, The Murre, Deep Water, High Jolly, Low Jolly, Louise's Rock, Humphrey's Rock, New Jolly, Westward Carn and East Carn Lee. I was so much used to these rocks that I could come up over them in the darkest hour of the night, and many times, after all my company have gone, I have stayed behind myself to catch a conger.

" Fifty years ago in Old Town there were between 40 and 50 strong able men, and they most of them got their living by labouring and fishing, piloting and making kilp. At that time, by making kilp in the summer season, men could get very good wages when it was a dry summer. The first kilp I can remember was £5 a ton, and almost every person on the island was working on it that summer. There are but three or four people on the island who can remember anything about kilp-making, so I will give you an account of how it is done. They would begin to make kilp in March month all around the island as soon as they could get any of the drift-weed in. They most commonly used to go two families together: there were but three of four horses and carts on the islands at that time and the seaweed used to be brought up in baskets by men, women and children, and every party had its own piece of ground to dry it on. The weed was spread and, if the weather was dry, in a day or two it was turned over, and when it was properly dry it was all made up in cocks, just like hay, above high-water mark where the sea could not come to it, and then the weed would be saved. After it had been in cocks for some time, and the weather being fine for burning it, they would have pits dug in the sand in the shape of a pan, quite small at the bottom and paved with small stones, and afterwards built around with single stones to a height of about two or three feet. The women would burn most of the kilp and the children would bring the weed to them while they were doing it, so that the men could do other work between times. All through the kilping season they would light up the kilp between eight or nine o'clock in the evening, putting on the weed in handfuls as fast as it would consume. After the kilp was burnt, six or eight men would come with kilp rakes to strike the kiln—that is, to work the kilp up— and when it was worked up it was like so much hot lead. They might have to work up as many as eight kilns, so they would have to run from one to another till they had completed all of them. There might be 40 or 50 kilns burning around St. Mary's in one day, so that each party would have to do its own work. The next morning a man would go down with a bar and raise the kilp up out of the pit; it would come out in a hard lump of about three-hundredweight: it was then broken up in handy lumps and put under the cliff, and the pit was cleared out for burning again the next day; and so they would continue their work till August month, getting as much seaweed as they possibly could. Everyone knew his own ground for drying the seaweed just the same as going in his fields to work.

" In the summer days kilp was being made on the six islands, and some days there would be as many as 100 kilns burning on the different islands. The smoke would come from the kilns as thick as it would from a steamer when new coals were put in: on a calm day the smoke would go straight up (a light smoke, almost white) and that would look grand.

" There were five kilp merchants on the island; they were all shopkeepers, selling groceries and drapery, so that all the people who worked about the kilp would go and take up anything they wanted. This work was finished in the middle of August and the kilp was then all shipped off to Bristol to make glass and soap. This work was carried on till the year 1835, when the last kilp was burned on the islands. Few persons made kilp that year and it was sold for 30s. per ton.

" The harvest now begins. There were fine crops of grain on the island at that time and every man and woman that could reap was employed to save the harvest: the grain was all cut with a reap-hook and the farmers were very particular as to how it was cut, especially the barley, which was spread thin on the ground so as to cover it all over in order to get it well dried. It was all used for making bread: they would leave it on the ground for six or seven days and then bind it and make it up in round mows in the fields and leave it for three or four weeks before bringing it into the mowhay. The main thing farmers looked for in those days was to get a good harvest and save their 12 months bread in good condition. The grain would all be got into the mowhays by the latter part of September and then they would begin to get up the late crop of potatoes. Every man and boy would be employed, just as they are in this day, getting out the early crop: men's wages were 1/6 a day and find themselves, or 1/3 a day and have meat at the house of the farm they were working on. They had their choice as to which they would take; men with families would take 1/6 a day and go to their own homes, as living was very cheap at that time. It was only 3d. a day for three good meals to the young men who used to have their meat where they worked, and I think they got the best of it at the end of the week.

" The potatoes were of much better quality than those grown at present and were sold for 2/- per bushel all the year round. Every labouring man who had no potatoes of his own would take in his winter's stock when he was digging—30 or 40 bushels, according to the number of his family—so that they should not fall short until the next crop. This was the way the work was carried on in St. Mary's until the disease got into the potatoes.

" Every family on the island used to have as much fish as they could make use of in the 12 months without any cost, except the salt to save them. Every man could go and catch his own fish after finishing his day's work, whatever his employment may have been.

" Every householder on the island, whether a farmer or not, kept some pigs, and a piece of ground by the house for growing potatoes to feed them. They would all have a pig to kill about Christmas-time, weighing from 16 to 18 score—pigs at that time being very large in the island; particularly about Old Town they would have them from 24 to 30 score weight, and their pork was better and sweeter than that of any of the small pigs killed in the present day. Pork was sold then for 3d. per pound by the side, and sometimes less; and best cuts of beef were sold on the market for 5d. per pound and other parts for less. The cattle were small, the average weight of a bullock being from 4 to 4½ cwt. The winter bullocks were all fed on potatoes with a little dry meal, and the beef was richer and had a better flavour than we get now. Veal sold for 3d., mutton for 3d. to 4d. per pound; young fowls for 1/- a pair; eggs 3d. to 4d. per dozen; and fresh butter 8d. pound.

" With the first strong breeze of wind we got from the east after the harvest, a great number of ships would come into the harbour. Vessels in those days were of a different class to those in use at present; they were not built to beat the wind but to sail before it, so that all the vessels that got into the Bristol Channel had to wait till the wind turned to the eastward before they could sail. When it came to a strong south-east wind they would all set sail, bound for the South Channel; when they came to the Land's

End they would all bear away for Scilly and come in a fleet.
I have known as many as 200 come in one day, reaching from
Giant's Castle up to the Roadstead, three and four abreast, which
was a grand sight; and after that vessels would be coming in every
day, while the wind was to the eastwards.

" The Roadstead, New Grimsby Harbour, Old Grimsby
Harbour and St. Helen's Pool would be as full of vessels as they
could hold; and these ships must have left a great deal of money
in the islands, as they had to lie there till the wind shifted to the
westward. If it changed on a fine day, all those vessels left the
harbour on that day: that is a sight we cannot see nowadays,
which is another great change that has taken place in 68 years.

" When we got east wind further on in the winter it was very
cold. The weather was very different 50 years ago to what it is now.
We used to get a great deal of calm weather, with the sun very hot,
and the hotter the summer, the colder was the winter. I have
known everything frozen up for three or four weeks at a time.
In cold winters there used to be a large number of wild fowls on
the islands. I have run around Peninnis on a cold morning to keep
myself warm and have put up as many as 20 cocks before break-
fast. In some cases they may have dropped and I may have put the
same bird up again, but woodcocks were very plentiful on the
islands at that time and, after heavy rain on the flat part of
Peninnis where shallow pools of water would stand, I could put
up hundreds of snipe every day. No person would fire at a snipe
in those days, so they were never disturbed unless anyone was
walking on the downs. A great quantity of wild geese and duck
used to come to this spot in the winter. Many people were in the
habit of walking around Peninnis to look at the vessels coming in,
and some would take their guns with them and shoot a goose or
duck, whichever they could fall in with. There were hundreds of
lapwing and plover on the islands, and everyone was allowed to
carry a gun who could buy one, but there were not many people
here who cared for much shooting.

" The summer of 1824 was the finest and pleasantest I ever
knew; in April, May and June we had fine, warm, pleasant
weather, with some showers to keep the crops growing. The
stems of the potatoes were three or four feet long that summer,
and there being no wind to hurt the crops, they grew as high as
five feet, and in many places higher than the hedges, so that when

two or three adjoining fields were in potatoes they looked like one field. When in bloom the potatoes carried a pink blossom, so that the islands looked like a flower garden.

" In 1825 occurred the season that was called the famine season, when everything was dried and burnt up by the hot sun—after heavy rain for one and a half hours in the latter part of May not a drop of rain fell till September. This occurred at a time when kilp was being made on the islands and most of the people working at it; they had a chance of keeping themselves cool by wading about in the sea during the hot weather. In the middle of the day the sand was so hot that nobody could stand on it for a moment. Several wells were dried up and also all the pools where the cattle drank, except a little in the lower moors, to which they were all driven. We had to fetch our water from Piper's Hole, at the head of Peninnis. The sun was so hot that summer that when the small pits were filled with water by the high tides, the water would be dried up and the salt left during the neap tides. I have gone down many times and scraped up 10 or 12 pounds that had been made by the sun, and you could get salt every neap tide through that summer. The hardest gale of wind that ever blew on the islands occurred on 13th February, 1833, from the westward. It was almost impossible for a man to stand on his legs, and we could not look to windward. A heavy rowing gig belonging to Tresco was up on the bank, and the force of the wind took her up in the air and the weight with which she came down broke her in pieces.

" It was thought that after the kilping was done away with people would not get any employment, but about that time ship-building began to go ahead on the islands. Small schooners were built for the fruit trade to St. Michael's and other ports and it was found to pay so well that they could not get men to build them fast enough; they had to get shipwrights from wherever they could. There were four master builders and all the young men were learning the shipwright business, which increased very fast; and shortly after that they began to build larger vessels for the Mediterranean and different parts of the world, and this trade was carried on for a great number of years. The shipowners had got some very fine vessels—large schooners, brigs and barques—trading in most parts of the world.

" The fleet of ships belonging to the Scilly Islands numbered between 60 and 70; the greater part of them were owned by the inhabitants, and it was said that they were paying thirty per cent. at that time. A shipping company was got up in £10 shares and did very well, and after that another was started in £5 shares, so that every person who had any money to lay out might have a chance of getting good interest for it. I belonged to the last company that was got up, and I believe most of the people on the islands who could raise £5 or £10 belonged to it to try their luck. There was £5,100 laid out in vessels, and after they had been running two years the accounts were made up, and owing either to bad captains or mistakes, the shares that were bought at £5 were only worth £2. Most of the small shareholders sold their shares at £2 and the company was broken up; but some of the large shareholders kept one of the vessels and ran her for a great number of years, almost bringing the shares up to £5 again.

" Since that time, as fast as shipping has got up it has gone down again. At one time there were nearly 70 ships belonging to Scilly, and now there is only one little coal vessel of 100 tons belonging to the port.

" It was about this time that they found out the market for early potatoes which brought high prices for a number of years. It was almost like coining money, and it was said that at that time the island was the richest place in the world for the number of people on it. It is not only the shipping that has failed, but every trade on the island. There is scarcely any work to do now. You will see many people standing about for want of work to do, who would willingly take any work they could get for low wages.

" The longest easterly wind I ever remember was in 1853; it commenced in February and lasted till the latter part of May, making between 13 and 14 weeks, with a great many strong breezes during the spring. There were nearly 100 sail of vessels lying in St. Mary's Roadstead in May and there was not a day they could get to sea.

" In 1854 we had a heavy storm of wind from the south-east; on the morning after the storm there was scarcely a green leaf to be seen on the island. Ten or twelve vessels were repaired on the island.

" In 1855 I engaged to work on the Trinity Works to build the lighthouse on the Bishop Rock. It was a very pleasant summer and I was much pleased with my employment. The labourers and bargemen were paid off on the last day of November, but the stone-cutters, carpenters and blacksmiths were all kept on three weeks later. The stones for the building were all worked in the yard on Rat Island. Shortly after I was paid off from this work I went to St. Agnes for a visit, and while on this island I met with a farmer who asked me if I would stay there and work for him all the winter. He had plenty of work for me to do till I wanted to ship on the Bishop works again, and I should lose no time as when it was not fit to work out of doors he had plenty for me to do in the barn. He offered me good wages, victuals and lodgings. There was plenty of money being got in St. Agnes at that time. The farmer belonged to one of the six pilot boats, and they were at sea every day in the winter when it was fit to go, and he was all behind with his work on the farm.

" I could not content myself on St. Agnes, but I was there all through the shortest days of the winter; they have five meals a day on this island . . . I worked on the Bishop works five years, and on St. Agnes each winter of that time."

VII

THE SMITH DYNASTY
AND THE FLOWER INDUSTRY

FOR NEARLY THREE YEARS FROM 1831 TO 1834, THE islands were directly under the Crown, and during this period the building of the church at Hugh Town was commenced and an extension of the pier to Rat Island was contemplated. Then in 1834 a member of an old Hertfordshire family, Augustus John Smith, leased the islands from the Crown for a period of three lives. In 1920 the terms of this lease were altered to enable the Duchy of Cornwall to carry out extensive improvements in the buildings and amenities of their property—it was said that some £70,000 was expended. Under the new terms, Tresco and the uninhabited islands were retained by the then representative of the Smith family, and the other islands came directly under the administration of the Duchy. Tresco was leased for 99 years from 1929.

Augustus Smith's rule was well suited to the needs of a community that had for years been struggling against economic difficulties without achieving any cohesion or settled plan, suffering from absentee proprietorship and a system of land tenure as unsatisfactory as could have been devised.[1] He completed, according to the terms of his lease, the new church building and the extension of the pier at Hugh Town; he built a house at Tresco, now called "The Abbey," alongside the ruins of St. Nicholas's Abbey; and he laid out the magnificent sub-tropical gardens which have become world-famous.

By virtue of land tenure, Augustus Smith ruled the Scillies as Lord Proprietor for 39 years. His tasks were to put some semblance of order into the lives of the inhabitants, and to find a solution to the apparently insoluble economic problems. His efforts were crowned with success.

[1] The law of majorats, or primogeniture, was not operative in the islands. On the death of a tenant his land was divided up amongst his children and, in consequence, the farms eventually became sub-divided into minute and scattered patches.

Tresco Abbey Gardens. The absence of severe frost enables sub-tropical vegetation to thrive in the open.

F

The wreck of the Earl of Lonsdale with Troy Town Maze, St. Agnes, in the foreground. This maze of small pebbles has been in existence well over a hundred years and was probably originally constructed by a bored lighthouse keeper.

Augustus Smith's first task was to put right an accumulation of abuses that had grown up following the rule (or misrule) of a succession of agents of the Godolphin-Osborne family. The situation demanded drastic action and a disturbance of the assumed vested rights and traditions of the inhabitants. His first action was to re-allot the farm lands so that each farmer had a sufficient and compact portion of suitable land to which the eldest son should succeed. The other children had to find other employment. There was plenty of work for those who were displaced by this re-arrangement of the tenancies and for all able-bodied men, for not only was the new addition to the pier and the work on the new church at Hugh Town completed, but new roads were constructed throughout the islands and the Lord Proprietor's residence commenced. Later, new schools were built on all the main islands and the attendance ensured by a levy of 3d. per week on all families who were in a position to send their children but who might neglect to do so. In effect, compulsory education was established in the Scillies thirty years before it became law on the mainland.

From 1834 until 1920, the Lord Proprietor (who was neither a lord nor, strictly speaking, the proprietor), exercised autocratic powers over all who lived on the islands. He not only controlled the tenancies but was chief magistrate and permanent chairman of the Council, which did not become truly elective till 1955.

Although the Council was nominally in control of police and licensing, the local policeman (sergeant by courtesy) was also game-warden and as such was a paid employee of the proprietor. In all practical matters the will of the proprietor prevailed.

Notwithstanding the fact that such a situation became less and less in accordance with democratic practice, it is questionable whether, considering the times and the place, any other system would have proved as beneficial in the long run. It was fortunate that, for the first time in their history, the islanders had the advantage of a series of proprietors who resided amongst them. Although authority was exercised arbitrarily, the system has been described, not without justification, as benevolent.

In the favourable and forward-looking climate established by Augustus Smith, the Scillonians themselves, without direct help from the Lord Proprietor, showed enterprise and self-help by organising and financing a great development of the local ship-building industry which had been initiated as early as 1825. By the middle of the nineteenth century there were no less than five ship-building yards at St. Mary's, and when the ships were built they were manned and skippered by Scillonians, and the ships and cargoes were the property of shareholders who were all islanders. To many, the coming and going of shipping afforded the opportunity of emigration to the colonies.

The Scillonian shipbuilding yards continued until about 1870, when wooden ships were being supplanted by iron. The largest was the "John Banfield", of 528 tons, and the growth of the industry may be judged from the following table:

Wooden ships registered in Scilly:

In 1825 there were	15	with a tonnage of		574	tons.
In 1838 ,,	,, 50	,,	,,	3,062	tons.
In 1851 ,,	,, 59	,,	,,	6,843	tons.
In 1864 ,,	,, 35	,,	,,	6,148	tons.

The Scillonian captains traded all over the world, though the majority were engaged in conveying potatoes and other freights.

Augustus Smith introduced new and better varieties of early potatoes to the islanders. He did not, however, confine his activities to the islands; he was also Liberal Member of Parliament for Truro from 1857–1865, and held many honorary positions in Cornwall. He died in 1872, and was succeeded by his nephew, Lieut. T. Algernon Smith-Dorrien, who then assumed by letters patent the additional name of Smith under the provisions of the will, and carried on the work initiated by his uncle for the welfare of the islands.

Lieut. T. Algernon Smith-Dorrien-Smith—the first "Smith" was later dropped—died in 1918 and was succeeded by his son, Major A. A. Dorrien-Smith, D.S.O., D.L., J.P., an acknowledged authority on botany and horticulture who was largely responsible for the development of the islands' successful trade in cut flowers. On his death in 1955 he was succeeded as lessee of Tresco and the uninhabited islands, by his son, Lt. Cdr. T. Dorrien-Smith.

The famous seven acre Abbey Gardens, Tresco, which are open to the public on weekdays, were laid out by Augustus Smith on the site of the Abbey of St. Nicholas, and have been enlarged and improved by successive members of the Dorrien-Smith family. Rare plants were obtained from all over the world, and the old

Scillonian sea captains in their voyages to the tropics brought back strange roots. The gardens are ideally sited and sheltered, and many tropical and sub-tropical plants flourish in the open; indeed, it is claimed that several botanical specimens have never been successfully cultivated elsewhere north of the Mediterranean in the open. In the gardens is a Valhalla of figureheads and carvings from some of the countless ships which have been wrecked in Scilly.

Nature provides the Isles of Scilly with a feast of colour all the year round, but especially in May and June when one may walk knee-deep over the springy cushions of thrift, with their masses of delicate pink blooms, and be dazzled by the blood-red splashes of sorrel and the golden trefoil and gorse. In the background, there is always the vivid blue sea that here rivals the Mediterranean and the Caribbean seas in the depth of its colour.

One of the commonest flowers on Scilly is the mesembri-anthemum, whose brilliant magenta and orange flowers are to be found in many cottage gardens and on walls. As though nature had not done enough, the islanders have planted every field of cultivable land with hedges of euonymus, veronica, escallonia or pittosporum in diminutive squares so as to present a chequer-board appearance. In these minute well-sheltered fields they cultivate the sixty million blooms that are exported annually to Covent Garden and provincial markets. The main varieties are the polyanthus narcissus (from December to May), iris, ixias, stocks and tulips. The equable climate, and the fact that frost is almost unknown, enables the Scillonian flower farmers to produce cut-blooms, cultivated in the open, considerably in advance of others except their rivals on the southern coasts of France. Some of the flowers are on the market in November or early in December.

The mainstay of the industry is the Soleil D'Or, a rich, yellow narcissus, with several flowers on each stalk and a strong scent. Together with the Paper White, it is one of the earliest to reach maturity. These varieties are followed by daffodils such as King Alfred and Fortune. The colour acquired by local grown flowers has never been equalled.

The origin of many of the bulbs of these flowers is wrapped in mystery. It is unlikely that they were indigenous; the Scilly White may have come from the South of France; the Paper White from Italy and Spain, and others from China. It is thought that the

earliest bulbs, the Scilly Whites, were brought by the monks of
St. Nicholas's Abbey and became naturalised on all the islands.
There is a local legend that the first bulbs were given to the wife
of a governor of Star Castle by a Dutch merchant captain in
return for some favour received. The lady, thinking they were
onions, boiled some and, not liking the taste, threw the remainder
into the castle moat, where they flourished.

The first Scillonian to pay any attention to these flowers which
were growing wild on St. Mary's, especially around the Garrison
and in the dry moat of Star Castle, was William Trevellick, who
for some years collected them secretly for his gardens at Rocky
Hill Farm. In or about the year 1881 an experimental consignment
of cut flowers was despatched to Covent Garden in, so it is said,
a hatbox, and, the resulting cheque being unexpectedly large, the
Scillonians were not slow to appreciate the possibilities. Mr.
Richard Mumford of Holy Vale, Mr. Hugh Watts and Mr. W. M.
Gluyas of Old Town, joined Mr. Trevellick and became the first
of the flower farmers.

The successful and permanent establishment of this industry was,
however, largely due to Mr. T. A. Dorrien-Smith, as will be seen
from the following statement, dated 1893, for submission to his
Royal Highness the Prince of Wales on behalf of the Trustees of
the late Mr. Augustus Smith:

" Mr. Dorrien-Smith . . . endeavoured to improve the cultivation
of early potatoes by the introduction of new seeds and fresh sorts;
but owing to foreign competition, their cultivation has proved to
be too hazardous and speculative for the Islanders to embark in to
any considerable extent.

" He next determined to introduce the cultivation of bulbs,
and with this in view he spent some time in Holland, studying the
system of cultivation there, and then imported by degrees large
quantities of them, selling them at cost price to his tenants. This
has now become a very popular and the most lucrative industry
there, and in favoured and sheltered spots can be successfully
carried on, and so long as the fashion of bulb flowers continues,
this industry promises to be a source of considerable profit to the
Islanders. But its introduction has cost Mr. Dorrien-Smith
£10,000, expended in the purchase of bulbs, the erection of bulb
and flower houses, etc. "

Mr. T. A. Dorrien-Smith went to Holland in the spring of 1882 and some 190 kinds of bulbs were planted in Tresco Abbey Gardens in the autumn of that year. He visited Messrs. Ware's grounds at Upper Tooting (then agricultural land) and also Messrs. Barr's nurseries, where many of the Incomparabilis, Barri and Ornatus hybrids were first raised—a few of these original kinds still exist in the Abbey Gardens but they have long since been surpassed by better types of market flowers.

In 1885 the Isles of Scilly Bulb and Flower Association was formed. Annual shows were held at St. Mary's and Mr. Dorrien-Smith presented a silver challenge cup for the best exhibit of cut flowers. The fashion for cut flowers in English households was revived in or about the year 1873 and has been maintained ever since.

The growth of the cut flower trade will be seen from the following table:

1881	one box realised £1		
1885	65 tons of cut flowers		
1886	85	,,	,,	,,
1887	100	,,	,,	,,
1889	198	,,	,,	,,
1896	514	,,	,,	,,
1924	700	,,	,,	,,
1931	1,064	,,	,,	,,

Later it exceeded 1,200 tons.

There is no doubt that the flower trade came just in time to save the islands from destitution, for it was introduced when the early potato harvests (which had been profitable since 1838) were failing, and when shipping and shipbuilding had come to an end. Today, the income received in the islands from the flower trade has been overtaken by a still more profitable industry, the tourist trade. Fortunately for Scilly the two trades are complementary rather than competitive, and the winter farmer turns in the summer into a boatman or a guest-house keeper so enabling him to have the best of both worlds.

VIII

WRECKS AND LOCAL CUSTOMS, ETC.

Methought I saw a thousand fearful wrecks;
A thousand men that fishes gnaw'd about;
Wedges of gold, great anchors, heaps of pearl,
inestimable stones, unvalued jewels,
All scatter'd in the bottom of the sea.

William Shakespeare,
(*Clarence's Dream, Richard III*).

THERE IS AN APOCRYPHAL STORY OF A SCILLONIAN addition to the Litany: "We pray Thee, O Lord, not that wrecks should happen, but that if any wrecks should happen, Thou wilt guide them into the Scilly Isles for the benefit of the poor inhabitants." There is another story of a clergyman of St. Agnes who, on being informed of a wreck whilst in the middle of delivering his sermon, announced it from the pulpit; on the next occasion of a wreck he said nothing, but walked to the church door and from there made his announcement, adding: "This time we all start fair!"

There is no doubt at all that the inhabitants of Scilly have benefitted considerably in the past from the frequency of wrecks around the islands, and they have not been slow to take advantage of what the elements have offered to them. The turbulent sea was so often the cause of their troubles[1] but sometimes, as in the case of a wreck, they were able to profit with advantage from other's misfortune. But there is no evidence to warrant accusations that Scillonians ever wilfully indulged in wrecking. Stories of cows left to wander on the coast with lights attached to their tails to confuse shipping have never been substantiated. But there is no doubt whatever that wrecks on Scilly were an intermittent, if not regular, source of income, and that in the course of time the islanders came to regard the proceeds of shipwrecks as part of their natural harvest. It is quite understandable that they should

---

[1] There was a rather grim local proverb that said: "For one who dies a natural death, nine are drowned." (Quoted by S. P. B. Mais in *Isles of the Island* p. 293).

have been recorded as objecting to the erection of a lighthouse—
" because it would rob them of ' God's Grace ' ", i.e. the produce
of wrecks.

The islands lie close to the track of main shipping routes, and
possess most formidable traps for the unwary mariner, including
variable currents and small unpretentious but deadly rocks often
wholly though insufficiently submerged. From America the
islands are the first landfall after a voyage of some 3,000 miles.
In the days of imperfect navigational instruments it is not surprising
that very many wrecks occurred.

Where Scillonians have distinguished themselves is not as
wreckers but as life-savers. With no hope or expectation of
reward, and solely at the dictates of humanity, Scillonian boatmen
have again and again risked, and often lost, their lives in attempting
to save the crews of shipwrecked vessels. From the seventeenth
century to the present day, over two hundred wrecks have
occurred on the Isles of Scilly, in many of which most of the
crews perished. Those sailors who preserved their lives often did
so because of the gallantry displayed by the islanders in rescuing
them.

The worst recorded disaster was that of Sir Cloudesley Shovel's
fleet in 1707, when, on the return journey from Toulon, five ships
struck on the Gilstone Rock, Scilly, and the flagship "Association"
and the large ships the " Eagle " and the " Romney " were lost with
all hands save only one man. About 2,000 men lost their lives. The
only survivor, from the " Romney ", saved himself by floating
on a piece of timber to the rock Hellweathers, where he remained
some days until he could be taken off. The body of Sir Cloudesley
was washed ashore at Porth Hellick, St. Mary's, where it was
buried, later to be disinterred and placed in Westminster Abbey
with great honour. Henry Trelawney also lost his life in this wreck;
he was the son of Bishop Trelawney, who was the hero of the
Cornish song:—

> "And shall Trelawney die?
> Then twenty thousand Cornish men
> Will know the reason why."

Amongst other naval vessels wrecked on the Scillies at different
times were the sloop " Lizard " (1747) in which a hundred men
perished; the " Colossus " (1777); and the brigantine " Foster "
(1833).

Of passenger steamers, the best known are the steam packet
" Thames " (1841), in which 62 persons lost their lives; the
" Delaware " (1871); the s.s. " Schiller " (1875), a mailboat from
New York to Bremen, in which 311 persons lost their lives; and
the s.s. " Minnehaha " (1910), which was afterwards refloated.

The stories of these wrecks produce some remarkable, almost
miraculous, accounts of persons who have been saved in spite of
the elements, but none so remarkable as that of the four men of
the brig " Nerina " of which the following is an account[1]:—

" The brig ' Nerina ', of Dunkerque, sailed from that place on
Saturday, the 31st October, 1840, under the command of Captain
Pierre Everaert, with a cargo of oil and canvas for Marseilles:
her burthen was about 114 tons; the crew consisted of seven
persons, including the captain and his nephew, a boy 14 years old.

"At three o'clock in the afternoon of Monday, the 16th of
November, they were forced to heave-to in a gale of wind at
about 10 or 12 leagues south-west of the Scilly Islands. At seven
o'clock of the same evening, still lying-to under their close-reefed
main-top-sail and balanced reefed main-sail, a heavy sea struck the
vessel and she suddenly capsized, *turning completely bottom up*.

" The mate succeeded in wrenching open the trap-hatch in the
cabin deck, and then he scrambled up into the vacant space and
took the boy from the hands of the captain, whom he assisted to
follow them.

" In about half an hour they were joined by Vincent and
Vantaure from the forecastle. There were then five individuals
closely cooped together; as they sat they were obliged to bend
their bodies for want of height above them, while the water
reached as high as their waists; from which irksome position one
at a time obtained some relief by stretching at full length on the
barrels in the hold, squeezing himself up close to the keelson.

" They were able to distinguish between day and night by the
light striking from above into the sea and being reflected up
through the cabin skylight, and then into the lazarette through
the trap-hatch in the cabin floor.

" The day and night of Tuesday, the 17th, and the day of
Wednesday, the 18th, passed without food, without relief, and
almost without hope; but still each encouraged the others, when

[1]   Quoted from L. C. Courtney's " Guide to Penzance "; from an account of the French
     Consular Agent, Penzance, 1840.

The launch of the David Auterson from Porthcressa, St. Mary's, in 1871. One of the last ships to be built in Scilly.

A storm in Hell Bay off Shipman Head, Bryher.

"The whole Atlantic
    Amassed recoils
And in indolent thunder
    Bursts and boils."

neither could hold out hope to himself, endeavouring to assuage the pangs of hunger by chewing the bark stripped off from the hoops of the casks. Want of fresh air threatening them with death by suffocation, the mate worked almost incessantly for two days and one night in endeavouring, with his knife, to cut a hole through the hull. Happily, the knife broke before he had succeeded in accomplishing his object, the result of which must have proved fatal, as the confined air alone preserved the vessel in a sufficiently buoyant state.

"In the dead of night of Wednesday, the 18th, the vessel suddenly struck heavily. Another hour or two of long suffering succeeded, when they were rejoiced to see by the dawning of the day of Thursday, the 19th, that the vessel was fast on rocks, one of which projected up through the skylight. The captain then went down into the cabin and found that the quarter of the ship was stoved and, looking through the opening, he called out to his companions above, ' Grace a Dieu, mes enfants, nous sommes sauvés ! Je vois un homme à terre '. Immediately after this the man approached and put in his hand, which the captain seized, almost as much to the terror of the poor man as to the intense delight of the captain. Several people of the neighbourhood were soon assembled; the side of the ship was cut open and the poor fellows were liberated from a floating sepulchre after an entombment of three days and three nights."

To reduce the dangers to shipping of the " rocks of Scilly ", the Master Wardens of the Guild or Brotherhood of the most Glorious and Undividable Trinity and of St. Clement, in the Parish Church of Deptford Strand, in the County of Kent, were granted by Letters Patent of King Charles II, dated 24th May, 1680 (32 Charles II), power and licence to erect and maintain one or more lighthouses upon any of the islands and to receive such allowance for maintenance of the same "as should be thought fit and reasonable according to law ".

St. Agnes' Lighthouse has the distinction of being the oldest but one of all the lighthouses in the British Isles, sometimes referred to as " the Land of Lighthouses ". The first was Winterton, in 1678; Scilly was the next, and Eddystone followed in 1694.

During 1679 and 1680, the 74 ft. circular white lighthouse on St. Agnes was built under the direction of Captain Hugh Till and Captain Symon Bayly. The first light was a coal fire lit in an iron brazier inside the lantern. It was very defective and not till 1807 was a satisfactory light installed. This consisted of thirty lamps burning spermaceti, magnified by reflectors, ten in each face of a triangular frame, with a circular motion. The payment of the light dues, when it was kindled, was most strongly opposed, and stringent measures had to be taken with many ships in order to enforce payment. The net revenue derived by the Trinity House from the St. Agnes' Light was £1,765 17s. 1d. in 1805, rising to £3,191 9s. 11d. in 1815.

The Bishop Rock and Eddystone are probably the two best known and certainly the two tallest lighthouses in the British Isles. Both are lone sentinels standing on pinnacles of rock almost submerged at high water. Both are graceful and stately towers, of delicate proportions yet, by reason of their weight, conveying the strength which they need to combat the highest seas. The Bishop shows a group flashing white light every fifteen seconds; in mist an explosive fog signal gives one report (similar to the discharge of a gun) every five minutes.

The Bishop was first constructed as an open structure of cast iron 120 feet high, but was washed away by a heavy sea on the night of February 5th, 1850, before it was ever used. A second structure, of stone, was built to replace it. It vibrated so much that in storms articles fell from shelves. This tower was strengthened in 1887 by building an outer casing round it and two extra stories were added, bringing it to its present height of 167 feet. This rebuilding cost £64,889 and took three years, and despite the hazardous nature of the undertaking, there were no recorded accidents. It was built by members of the Douglass family, and William Tregarthen Douglass, who completed it, was the son of Sir James Douglas F.R.S., engineer-in-chief of Trinity House, who married a Scillonian, the daughter of Captain James Tregarthen.

In 1911 a lighthouse was built on Peninnis Head, giving a white flash every fifteen seconds, to take the place of St. Agnes' Light which was discontinued. No keepers are resident. The 63 ft. high circular lighthouse built on the 3 acres of Round Island shows a flashing red light every half-minute. The light is 180 ft. above high water and can be seen for twenty miles in clear visibility. It was built in 1887. In mist, a siren is sounded every two minutes.

As many as eight light beams can be seen from Telegraph Hill on a clear night. At Seven Stones is anchored a lightship; to the north-east is the Longships, and Pendeen; and to the east is the Wolf and the powerful Lizard Light. To aid navigation today there is every modern assistance such as beam radio, and older devices such as the bell-buoy to mark the approaches to the Spanish Ledges.

Smuggling by its nature being a secretive enterprise, it is very difficult to estimate the amount that Scillonians have participated in it in the past. Certainly in the 18th century (the great age of smuggling) Scilly provided a most suitable base for the traffic, and Jessie Mothersole, in a chapter entitled " Former Industries ", says that smuggling was a very popular employment and that even the clergy engaged in it. She instances a report, we know not on what foundation, that the Rev. John Troutbeck, who wrote his book on Scilly in 1794, had to leave the islands " from fear of the consequences of having taken part in it ".

In Scilly, as elsewhere, the growth in this century of the scientific attitude, and the success of modern education in fostering it, has been steadily destroying the vast system of folklore and superstition by which people used to live. But in Scilly, as in most sea-faring communities, the remnants of omens and charms still linger tenaciously, if sometimes ludicrously, particularly those connected with the sea and ships. It is said for instance to be difficult to persuade a Scillonian to change the name of his boat, however inappropriate the name may be, because doing so might bring bad luck to the boat and those who went in her. In the days of sail, there used to be a whole series of taboos connected with boats but the greater safety afforded by the internal combustion engine must have played its part in ending them. It was advisable, when at sea, never to mention any land animal, especially a rabbit; nor to count fish as they were being hauled aboard; nor to whistle unless it was calm—" there is wind enough! " A gale was thought inevitable if a parson was aboard, and if the dinghy had to be turned round this must be done in a clock-wise direction.

Amongst the customs that survive is that of crowning the May Queen on May Day, followed by song and dance around the maypole erected in the park in the centre of Hugh Town. The Queen, attended by her guard and maids of honour, parades through the town, the streets of which are littered with gorse petals and flowers which have been gathered by the children for the occasion. In olden times, May whistles cut from alder or sycamore branches, and the blowing of cow-horns, added to the fun. May Day was a general holiday and fishing boats from Newlyn would come over and the fishermen would join in the singing and merriment. In the morning all the children walked to selected farms where they were given a round of bread, thick cream and black treacle. (A round of bread, on Scilly, is equivalent to a slice of bread whereas a slice is equal to half-a-slice on the mainland. No bread boards are used and the loaf, held in the hand, is cut towards the body: round for a " round " and then commencing beyond the centre and cutting inwards with increasing depth, for a " slice ". Symmetry is restored by reversing the loaf for the second slice). Today's festivals include a Carnival Queen who is elected in August followed by a procession of decorated vehicles and plenty of comic set pieces. There is also an annual regatta including water sports with traditional diversions such as " walking the greasy pole ".

In previous centuries, Harvest Festivals, termed " Nicla-Thies " occurred after the last of the grain had been gathered and were accompanied by much feasting. On the near approach of Christmas, the Goose-dancers (a survival of Morris-dancers), Merry Maskers or Guise-dancers, made their appearance. Maidens dressed up as men, sometimes in ship captains' uniforms and men in women's costumes would parade through the town. Some of the men and women would dress in parti-coloured costume, " half of one colour to the right and left, or above and below ", says Heath. The children would blacken their faces or don hideous masks. On Shrove Tuesday the boys had a right to throw stones in the evening against the doors of dwelling houses. They could be bought off with pancakes or money. This night was called " Gravel-Night " and the stones, which were collected from the beaches, were about the size of small marbles. The custom of going limpeting on Good Friday, according to Jessie Mothersole, still continued in 1914 and may still not have entirely died out. In addition to limpets, the islanders collected winkles and a kind of rockling always called " whistlers ". They are said to be very tasty and are found under beach stones. On Good Friday young and old made a point of releasing paper boats on the water. The origin of this custom is unknown and it may be a votive offering to the gods of the sea. In addition to paper boats there were regular model-boat racing competitions across the pools. The boats used were the pride of their constructors and were fully rigged and up to four feet long.

An annual fair was held in the park of Hugh Town on Whit-Mondays. Midsummer Night was " Tar Barrel Night " when blazing torches were carried and bonfires set going. Tar barrels, stove in at the tops, and alight, were carried in procession on men's heads. The flames would leap up eight or more feet and molten tar fall on the bearers who had to choose their moments for dropping their loads. On the 5th November the boys of St. Mary's had a holiday called " Ringing Tide " part of which day they spent in ringing the church bells. Trips to Penzance were rare, but Whit-Monday was the great excursion day and, in 1914, cost 3/6d. return. An annual day picnic to Samson is still maintained and islanders on St. Mary's are still great picnickers. Pelistry Bay, St. Mary's, is well patronised by them on fine Sundays in the summer months.

Of legends, that of the so-called " Saint " Warna is the most persistent. St. Warna was supposed to be an Irish saint who landed in a coracle on St. Warna's Bay, St. Agnes, and possessed the power of attracting ships to their doom. The people of St. Agnes were said to propitiate the " Saint " and invoke her aid during poor wrecking seasons by dropping pins into her " well " on the day after Twelfth Day. Others claim that St. Warna's Bay is a corruption of " Santa Juana ", a Spanish ship said to have been wrecked there.

There is a proverb, quoted by Jessie Mothersole:
 " Southerly wind and fog
 Easterly wind all snug."

Of fancies, it is said that a cat lying in front of the fire with its tail turned to the north is an indication of a gale of wind. The granite in Hugh Town is claimed to possess the property of glistening early in the morning in advance of fine weather, whereas when it is dull, a storm may be expected.

Dancing is frequently mentioned in the records, but only one seems to have any local flavour, which it shares with West Cornwall, the Phoebe (Phoebe or Phibbie was the Moon Goddess):

" Cannot you dance the Phoebe,
Don't you see how my shoulders shake,
Don't you see what pains I take,
Cannot you dance the Phoebe? "

Of superstition, we are informed by Whitfield (1852) that
Tresco " swarmed " with witches, and Heath (1750) says that it
cannot be expected that these islands should be quite free of
delusions. " Some few here imagine (but mostly old women) that
women with child, and the first born, are exempted from the
power of witchcraft; and tell you a story of a bewitching woman,
that bewitched a man with blindness who refused her a pin . . .
Fairies are said to have frequented Buzza Hill on St. Mary's
Island, but their nightly pranks, aerial Gambols and Cockle-Shell
Abodes are now quite unknown. Haunted Houses, Giants and
Apparitions (so terrible in Scilly some years ago) are now, by
application made to the Knowing Men of Cornwall, all charm'd,
cast in a Spell, or conjur'd out of the Islands."

Of medical practice in his time, Heath says: " For want of Male
practitioners in Physic, the few diseases and hurts in these healthful
Islands have, for these many years past, been remedied by a
' Society of Skilful Aunts ', constituting a sort of College of
Physicians in Scilly, of which Aunt Sarah is the Head or President
. . . When they assemble upon a woeful, desperate or doubtful
case, they resign the patient to God and Nature, while the
attending Doctress provides a warm room, a nurse, and fit
necessaries, which co-operate with uncommon success. Common
diseases here (not proceeding from Luxury, Laziness and Intem-
perance) are cured by one of the subordinate practitioners with a
few Simples, without calling in the assistance and judgment of a
second or third graduate.

" They have some disguised Nostrums and Specificks, the true
Secrets of which Compositions are deposited with their President
. . . Mrs. Sarah Jenkins (commonly called Aunt Sarah) . . . a
person of singular skill and circumstance, she does many acts of
charity and benevolence to the poor-distressed; to which the rest
of the younger sisterhood, who are not a little amiable, contribute
their parts. The president is remarkable for her venerable long
beard, which some imagine operates miraculously to the Benefit
of those who stroke it."

Heath was the first chronicler to pay any special attention to the Scillonian people as such, excusing himself by saying: " I consider that the little oddities in the customs and manners of the lower class of people are not without amusement and instruction. Here truth appears in its natural simplicity, unadorned with meretricious embellishments, and beautiful in its own nakedness. Honour, Justice and every social virtue is exercised among them in the strictest punctuality, though there is never a lawyer and but one clergyman, in all the Islands ".

After Heath's time, there were several clergymen who wrote accounts of the islands, the Rev. John Troutbeck (1794) being followed by the Rev. G. Woodley (1822). Woodley commences by soundly rating Troutbeck and Heath, saying: " In a word, Heath's Account may be read once for curiosity but will never be referred to with pleasure ".

Of the products of the soil, Woodley tells us that wheat, barley, pillas and potatoes were grown—pillas was a kind of wild or " naked " oats—and of the cattle he says that they were black and small, and in the off-islands, were fed in a great measure on seaweed. Horses, he adds, were small and generally poor, " their chief food is the furze which they find on the hills, and which they carefully bruise with the forehoof before manducation; yet I have been assured that both cows and horses, by custom, acquire such a relish for these peculiar and piquant articles of food, that they pine when deprived of them ".

An interesting fishing procedure, still operated in the traditional manner at low tides on St. Martin's Flats and around Samson is, that of clapping the hands. The scallops, lying under the wet sand, respond to the claps by closing their shells sharply thus emitting a jet of water upwards and disclosing their location.

An old manuscript, dated 1695, mentions the following curious custom: " In all these Islands they take a sort of fish about a foot in length, by angling upon the shore. This they call the ' Whistling Fish ' and giving it that name because they whistle whilst they take it, this fish rarely taking the bait unless they doe, for whereas if the anglers whistle and make a vocal noise (which they usually do alternately) they bite very freely.

The manuscript continues: " In the Islands of St. Martin and St. Mary they have a sort of bituminous earth in great plenty. They use it for fire and indeed burnes very well only it emits a sulphurous smell. 'Tis the only fewell they have, there being no coal nor any trees, not soe much as a shrubb, except brambles, furzes, broom and holly; and these never grow above four foot high . . . "

" . . . shipwrecks are very frequent. These the inhabitants call God's Blessings, they have a third part of all the goods they can save allowed by the proprietors of the ship, unless they hire ye assistance of the Islanders at such a determinate price to save all they can. In case all the men on board be cast away then all they can save is their owne."

Of the customs of the mid-eighteenth century, Heath reminds us of the proverb "Always a feast or a famine in Scilly", and that they had a very plentiful feast after harvest time called Nicla Thies. Heath summarises the detached and independent nature of the islands in his time in the following paragraph:

" No Islander is a freeholder, no person has a vote for choosing members of Parliament, nor are the islands represented by any, which shew that they are no part of the Country or County jurisdiction of Cornwall, but are distinct from both under a separate government. Here is no prison for the confinement of offenders, which shews that the people live upright enough not to require any, or that the place is a confinement of itself." His comment on the drinking habits of the islands is " most of the private are public houses ", and he complains frequently of the poor quality of the locally brewed beer, which, in his time, was 2d. a quart.

Of burials, Heath says that " when an islander dies, some friends sit up the night with the dead, where it is a custom with them to feast cheerfully during the time . . . after the burial they express great concern for the loss of their friend, whom they lament is no more to be seen. The Chaplain performs the service and is well paid for his performance and claims, by the right of his office, a Scarf."

Of matrimony, he records that fifty years before his time banns were called and the chaplain paid five shillings, or not above half-a-guinea—or he would take what he could get. " Soldiers and persons, at that time, not in circumstances to pay for being joined, either joined themselves, or were joined gratis, i.e. they were joined by vows, or taking one another's word, which was binding as long as they could agree. And this sort of conscientious binding was observed to hold as fast, and be as good a security of their future felicity, as if the parties had been tied together with the sacred shreds of matrimony."

Woodley, in 1822, seems to have nurtured a few grievances against the islanders; he complains of the difficulty of obtaining labour, particularly domestic, " because the women preferred kelping or knitting ", and he comments unfavourably on the finery (straw hats and flying ribands) displayed on Sundays, which he thinks " ludicrous " by contrast with the week-day lack of shoes or stockings. He also speaks of the exorbitant charges " for any little service ", but subsequent writers refute this statement and suggest that the islanders had a special price for the Rev. G. Woodley. One observation he makes is revealing: " there is an affected degree of independence amongst the Islanders, which even the pressure of poverty and affliction is unable to subdue." This independence he refers to as " this sort of Spanish feeling ".

The military and ecclesiastical history of the islands up to the eighteenth century gives us very little information regarding the inhabitants, who were ruled by the Abbot and military governors and by the stewards of the absentee landlords. From the time of Elizabeth to the refusal of the Duke of Leeds to renew his lease in 1831 when the islands reverted to the Crown, tenure was short so that there was little security or encouragement to accumulate family fortunes in buildings or farmland.

After the Dissolution, the ecclesiastical administration of the islands was somewhat anomalous, and it was not until 1836 that the islands were declared by Act of Parliament to be within the jurisdiction of the Bishop of Exeter. In the year 1660 the church at Old Town, St. Mary's, was constructed on the site of an older Norman structure, and when this fell into decay the new church at Hugh Town was constructed, and completed in 1838. In Tresco there was a small church whose origin is shrouded in uncertainty, but which existed in 1798. It was enlarged in 1824 and 1835, and finally replaced by the present church in 1879. Bryher had its church in 1742, which was enlarged in 1928. The church on St. Martin's was enlarged in 1790 and restored early in the nineteenth century. A church on St. Agnes was erected sometime in the sixteenth or seventeenth century and destroyed in a gale. In the eighteenth century a second church was constructed by the inhabitants from the proceeds of wreck and salvage. This also was destroyed and the present church was erected early in the nineteenth century, and its roof was recently renewed.

There has been an Anglican clergyman resident on St. Mary's since 1662. But in Heath's time (1750), he had neither institution, induction nor visitation from the Bishop. He held his appointment from the Lord Proprietor, and received the keys from his Agent. The off-islands have had curates only since 1842; previous to which date they were served mainly by laymen. The Society for Promoting Christian Knowledge founded "The Scilly Mission" in 1765, and continued to supply missionaries to the off-islands until 1842 both for religious instruction and secular education. Schools were built on St. Martin's and St. Agnes in 1830.

A Roman Catholic church was built near the present harbour in 1840 and dedicated to St. Martin. In 1844, the Baptist Society came to Scilly and flourished until the late 1840's, when its activities ceased owing to a controversy amongst the members. The Bible Christian Society established itself in 1821, and in the following year numbered 144 adherents. Chapels were constructed in St. Mary's and in St. Martin's in 1823, and in St. Agnes in 1832. In 1827 Mr. William O'Bryan visited Scilly and the members of the Society afterwards became known as Bryanites. The United Methodist Society, the United Free Church and the Methodist New Connexion amalgamated in 1907 to form the United Methodist Society, and the final reunion, Wesleyan Methodist Church, the Primitive Methodist Church, and the United Methodist Church was formally sealed in 1932.

Woodley, speaking of religion in his time (1822), says that the Scillonians' behaviour at church was decent and exemplary: "They pay such attention to the external duties of religion that in St. Mary's and Tresco, where dissenters have established themselves, many of the people, halting between two opinions, repair to the meeting-house in the morning, to Church in the forenoons and afternoons, and again to the Meeting in the evening." Sundays were so very crowded with services of one kind and another that the Sunday School had, at one time, to be held on Saturday afternoons.

John Wesley visited the isles in 1743 in a boat borrowed from the Mayor of St. Ives, and the Society was established later in

1788. In 1792, the membership reached 150. The original chapel was erected in 1790, and the existing one completed in 1828.

Of royalty who have visited the islands, the earliest record is of King Athelstan, in A.D. 936, followed by King Olaf Trygvasson; Svein Ashifahson, " King of Orkney and Caithness "; Charles I, when Prince of Wales; his son, Prince Charles (afterwards Charles II); Queen Victoria, with Prince Albert and the Prince of Wales, in 1847; King Edward VII in 1902; King George V (when a midshipman); Edward, Prince of Wales, in 1921, and again in 1933.

Queen Victoria's visit was unexpected, but she was received with due ceremony and drove through Hugh Town and up to Star Castle. On the return journey the coachman mistook the way and commenced to descend the steep hill from the Garrison Gateway to the Town. One of the horses stumbled and alarmed the Royal party—it is said that the Queen's nerves had been shaken by an attempt on her life a short time previously—and she alighted and completed the journey on foot.

The Prince of Wales (later King Edward VIII and the Duke of Windsor) came to Scilly by seaplane from Falmouth in May, 1933. His Royal Highness was entertained to lunch at Star Castle.

Since the 2nd World War Queen Elizabeth, the Queen Mother, and the Duke of Edinburgh made visits to Scilly, and were welcomed most enthusiastically by the islanders.

APPENDIX

I. CLIMATE

The Isles of Scilly enjoy an equable climate with less variation between day and night temperatures than in large land areas. The range of mean monthly temperatures in a year, taken over a number of years, is 15.4 degrees Fahrenheit as compared with Montpellier (French Riviera) 31.1 degrees, and Pau 32.2 degrees. The range is actually less in Scilly than in Nice or Algiers. The mean temperature for the coolest month of the year is 46 degrees Fahrenheit as compared with 46 degrees for Nice, 46 for Barcelona and 41 for Bordeaux. In winter, it may be claimed, therefore, that Scilly is as warm as the Mediterranean Riviera. In normal winters frost and snow are entirely absent.

In summer it never becomes sultry in Scilly because there is always some breeze off the sea on a sunny day. Rainfall is not excessive and thunderstorms are rarely severe. Winds, however, can be high, especially in the autumn and winter.

It is said of the Scillonian climate that visitors in the summer months who are unfortunate enough to encounter a spell of bad weather, can console themselves with the thought that, however inclement it may be in Scilly, it is nearly always worse on the mainland of England.

II. BIRDS

Scilly is famous as a breeding place of seabirds, and as a halting place in spring and autumn for many rare migrants including some which manage to cross the 3000 miles of open ocean between Scilly and America. The common land birds of the islands are all familiar British species. It is on the water, and along the coasts, that the most interesting birds will be found. They fall into five main groups—cormorants, gulls, auks, petrels and waders.

Of the cormorants, the shag is the more widespread and common. It is rather like a large greenish-black duck with a long snaky neck, which swims very low in the water and dives freely.

In spring it has a graceful crest. The common cormorant is actually more scarce in Scilly than the shag, and is chiefly found on and near the outer islands. It is reputed to consume an average of 7 lb. of fish each day. It is much longer, blacker and more heavily built, and in some plumages it shows a good deal of white, which the shag never does. Both these birds have the odd habit of standing on a rock with wings outspread giving a gargoyle-like effect.

The gannet is usually seen cruising gracefully from twenty to a hundred feet above the water. It is a large white bird, with black wing tips and a buffish head, and has a spectacular habit of diving after fish from a considerable height, making a great splash. Its nearest breeding colony is Grassholm off Pembrokeshire.

One of the most characteristic Scilly birds is the greater black-backed gull, which is as big as a goose and more destructive to wild life than most birds of prey. A fully grown bird may have a wing span of up to six feet. It is a great killer of puffins and shearwaters. White, with long, black wings and a savage, yellow and red bill, it is seen on all the islands and nearby waters. It is liable to dive upon and attack people who interfere with its eggs in the nesting colonies. It came to Scilly late in the 19th century. The lesser black-backed gull can be distinguished by its slaty-grey (instead of black) wings, and its yellow (instead of pink) legs. The third common species of gull in the islands is the herring gull, which has a much lighter, pearl-grey mantle and wings; it is very tame locally and is fond of sitting on houses or the masts of boats. It is not generally appreciated to what age seagulls may attain. Recent results from ringing have established that individual birds live up to thirty or more years.

The kittiwake is a small oceanic gull which frequently crosses the Atlantic, occasionally nesting in small numbers on the outer rocks. Its distinctive mark is a grey wing with no white " window " on its triangular black tip. A smaller, more graceful relative is the slender, swallow-like common tern, often seen diving for fish in shallow waters. The roseate tern, perhaps the most delightful to watch of all sea birds, is happily returning to the islands in fair numbers, breeding especially on Annet.

By far the commonest auk is the razorbill which looks like a small plump penguin, black above and pure white below, with a large, deep, black bill, crossed by a white line. In the water it swims high and dives freely. It flies with very rapid wing beats, and often in strings of a dozen or more birds together. It lays a single egg on rock ledges, and sits on it in an upright, standing posture. The browner, dagger-billed guillemot has similar habits, but is scarcer in Scilly. Colonies of guillemots have the peculiarity of possessing a proportion with special markings—the bridled guillemots. The further south the colony the fewer are found with these markings, and in Scilly about two in every hundred may be discovered. The markings consist of a white line round the eye continuing backwards on each side of the head towards the nape of the neck.

The smaller, plumper puffin breeds in burrows on Annet and two or three other islands. It is the clown of sea birds, and flies apparently only with the greatest difficulty. Its take-off involves vigorous propulsive beating of the sea with its wings, causing cascades of spray in all directions in its efforts to achieve enough lift to become air-borne. Landing is equally comical to the human eye, completely lacking in the self assurance normally associated with the flight of sea-birds. Flight being difficult, it usually contrives to escape from enemies such as the greater black-backed gull by diving below the surface of the sea, beating its wings to propel itself along under water. Its most outstanding feature is its multi-coloured parrot-like bill which looks quite artificial set on its white face with red-rimmed eyes.

The petrels, relatives of the albatross, are the most oceanic of birds, only coming to land to breed. The manx shearwater has its only English breeding colony in Scilly. It is a fascinating and mysterious bird, blackish above and silky-white below, with the typical tube-nosed bill of its order. Terror of the greater black-backed gulls leads it to enter and leave its nesting burrow only during hours of darkness, when its strange crowing calls can be heard on all sides. It thinks nothing of going off hundreds of miles on a flying expedition, which may take it away from the nest for days, and every summer it abandons its young before they can fly. Its name comes from its strong, easy, unmistakable flight, never more than a few feet above the water, canting first to one side and then to the other, so that the black upper and white lower parts show alternately.

The larger, whitish fulmar petrel has lately begun to colonise Scilly in small numbers. It nests in the open on cliffs, and defends itself against interference by squirting over intruders an oily liquid whose unpleasant smell persists almost indefinitely. The storm-petrel, or mother carey's chicken, also nests in Scilly, but is nocturnal and unlikely to be seen.

Of land birds the most unusual are the shore-loving rock-pipit, a greyish brown bird, which has a remarkable parachuting song-flight; and the gorse-loving stonechat, the male of which is a handsome, plump little bird with a black head, an orange breast and long, white panels in its brown wings. The islands are remarkable for not having any breeding woodpeckers, owls, buntings or wagtails, and only a single species of crow—the raven.

Only two species of wader breed in the islands, the ringed plover with its hurried walk, and the handsome black and white oystercatcher. The oystercatcher's most distinctive feature is a bright orange bill over three inches long. Most of the tidal rocks on Scilly are covered with limpets which are not hard to dislodge at the first blow, but subsequent attacks only serve to tighten their hold, and indeed the shell of the limpet will break before its grip will loosen. But the Oystercatcher has developed a technique for dealing with such crustaceons (including oysters as its name implies) and its long bill is ideal for picking and probing for eggs, worms and similar morcels.

Wild life on Scilly enjoys some protection. The island of Annet, which is the principal island for the breeding of sea birds, is closed for landings between April 15th and July 20th except for scientific research. The islands of Melledgan, Gorregan, Rosevean, Scilly Rock, Green Island off Samson, Mincarlo, and Menavaur require permits for landing in the close season, and these are issued by the Honorary Warden on behalf of the Nature Conservancy and are strictly controlled. The taking or destroying of the eggs of any wild birds is prohibited, and only those specially appointed are allowed to shoot birds. With the wholehearted co-operation of boatmen and islanders generally, wildlife is flourishing. A bird observatory started on St. Agnes in 1959 has produced some interesting new knowledge about bird migration.

III. FAUNA (other than birds)

Owing to the shortage of sheltered land not already claimed for bulb culture or vegetable growing, there are few domestic farm animals on the islands except cows. It is long since deer roamed the Garrison and Samson, and there are no sheep now on any of the islands.[1] No licence is required to keep a dog and there are plenty on St. Mary's but few on the off-islands. Cats are prolific, however. There are few varieties of wild animals though black rabbits can be found on Samson and white ones on St. Helen's.

Because of the relatively mild climate some of the fauna of the Isles of Scilly show a closer connection with the fauna of the warmer parts of Europe than with the rest of the British Isles. For example, the Scilly Shrew (*Crocidura Cassiteridum*) is unique; it is not found at all in other parts of the British Isles, but a closely related species is found in France. There is also a species of grasshopper found in the Isles of Scilly which also occurs in France but not in other parts of the British Isles.

Among the mammals of the Isles of Scilly besides the common porpoise, common dolphin, grey seal, rabbit, and Scilly shrew, can be found the long-tailed field mouse, house mouse, brown rat, pipistrelle bat, and long-eared bat. The red deer, roe deer, and Hebridean vole are now extinct in the islands.

Some fairly common species are missing from the islands. For example, there are no foxes, badgers, moles, hedgehogs, stoats, weasels, snakes, hares and not many wasps.

Porpoises are sometimes seen around the islands and frequently near the boats, particularly the quiet sailing craft rather than the noisy motor launches. Dolphins in occasional large schools are an impressive sight owing to their habit of leaping twice their height out of the water. The huge but lethargic basking shark is frequently seen, often over twenty feet in length and it can grow up to forty feet. Its dorsal fin, cutting through the water, is clearly visible above the surface as the shark glides serenely by, and can be quite alarming to anyone unfamiliar with the fact that, huge as it is, this shark feeds on minute organisms only, and is of no danger at all to bathers.

Colonies of grey seals are to be found on the northern, eastern and particularly on the western rocks of Scilly. At low water they are often observed basking on the rocks, but, when approached,

---

[1] There were plenty of sheep in the 18th century. Woodley relates that Top Carn, St. Martin's, was struck by a thunderbolt on 20th November, 1751, and a horse and up to sixty sheep were killed.

slide off into the sea where their heads, resembling those of large dogs, keep bobbing up as they watch the intruding boat.

The grey seal, which is the largest mammal to breed wild in the British Isles, grows to a length of up to eight feet and is found only in the Atlantic and the seas of northern Europe. The seal pup is less than three feet long when born and looks most attractive in its creamy white fur; but by the end of its first three weeks of life it is deserted by its mother who will no longer suckle it and it is left to fend for itself. By the end of the fourth week it will have moulted and lost all its fur. The cows often live to thirty-five years and more, but the bulls rarely live over twenty years.

IV PLACE NAMES AND DIALECT

Before the 16th century the language in Scilly was the Celtic dialect of Cornwall. It survives in place-names like *Agnes, Tresco, Bryher, Annet, Ganilly*; and in many names of rocks. *Men* (rock) occurs in *Menavaur, Menawethan, Mincarlo, Muncoy, Melledgan, Tolman* etc. The Cornish word for a bay or inlet was *porth*, as in *Porthcressa* and *Porth Mellon* (Mill-Bay) where the earliest mill stood. There are many variations: *Per Conger, Pelistry, Periglis* or *Priglis* (Church Bay); and the common word *par* (inlet). Some of the Celtic names are intelligible: *Tresco* is *tre* (farm) and *scaw* (elderbushes); *Bryher* is *bre* (hill) and *har* (big); *Innisidgen* is Innis-i-Geon (John's Island); in *Rosevear* and *Rosevean, vear* means "big", *vean* "little" and *Rose* something like "high waste land". Many are hopelessly corrupted. A Bryher man will say *Elzwilzick* for the island that modern maps call *Illiswilgig;* but old maps have *Inaswittick*, so that the first part was *innis* (island). The meanings of *Scilly* itself, *Agnes, Annet, Ennor* (the old name of St. Mary's) and most other Celtic names are unknown. In Celtic names the defining word usually comes second and is accented, e.g. Carn Néar, Porth Héllick (Willow Bay), Penínnis (island head). Contrast English names like Húgh Town, Búzza Hill (from the surname Bosow), and Bánts Carn.

Celtic died out in Cornwall during the 18th century. In Scilly, where fresh garrisons and settlers were constantly coming from

H

England, it was given up earlier, and visitors were often surprised at the good English spoken by Scillonians. Some features of Cornish English are found: "Where's he to?", "Over to Bryher"; "He do belong (or he belongs) to be early," meaning "he is usually early". A *Troy-Town* or *High-Goal* is a "confusion", or "mess". Some English words have unusual meanings: *nothing rash* (of the weather), "nothing violent"; *to be frightened*, "to be surprised"; *to be jealous of*, "to distrust". In Scilly the ordinary rowing boat is called a *punt*. Common words connected with fish or fishing are: *corb* (or *carb*), the floating box in which live lobsters, crawfish and crabs are stored; *wra-pot*, a close-meshed lobster-pot baited for wrasse; *hector*, the in-shore crab; *garlops*, the blennies that small boys fish for. Less common are *gerricks*, garfish, *whistler* and *pettifox*, kinds of rockling. Of sea birds *merrick* is the tern, *cockathoden* the shearwater. A *ledge* is a patch of rock that is usually submerged. On land, field-walls of loose stone are called *hedges*; green hedges, which are recent, are always *fences*. The general name for daffodils is *lilies*; but a grower names varieties exactly. e.g. Fortune, and shortens long names, e.g. *Sols* for Soleil d'Or, *Mags* for Magnificence. Bulbs are usually called *roots*; the roots of plants are *mores*; *vore* means "furrow", *teal* "to plant".

V POPULATION[1] AND ACREAGES

	Acreage	Population (1951)	Population (1961)
Inhabited Islands	4,041	2,194	2,288
St. Mary's	1,611	1,625	1,736
Tresco	962	243	283
St. Martin's	682	131	118
St. Agnes and Gugh	433	78	85
Bryher	353	117	66
Samson	120	nil	nil
St. Helens	80	nil	nil
Teän	70	nil	nil

[1] Figures include visitors

Population figures of residents in the Isles of Scilly (excluding the military) have been computed from various sources as follows:

Date	Population
1700	1000
1750	1400
1814	2358
1932	1631
1950	1885
1951 (8th April)	1880
(2194 including visitors)	
1960	1820
1961 (23rd April)	1800
(2288 including visitors)	
1963 (30th June)	1790

VI CHRONOLOGICAL SUMMARY
EXCERPTS FROM RECORDED HISTORY

A.D.

384 The Emperor Maximus banished Bishops Instantius and Tiberianus to " Insula Sylina " for heresy.

400—1100 Christian hermits; probably on all the main islands. The best known was St. Elid—who lived on St. Helen's.

800—1570 Scilly a base for pirates.

990 An old saga relates that the Viking, Olaf Tryggvason, came to Scilly with nearly a hundred ships and, during his stay, was converted to Christianity—possibly by St. Elid. Olaf took with him from Scilly " priests and other learned men " and introduced Christianity to Norway and Iceland.

1114 Henry I granted Tresco and neighbouring islands to the Abbey of Tavistock and a Benedictine priory, St. Nicholas, was established on Tresco.

1284 Drew de Barrentine sent by Henry III as Governor of the Islands.

1306   Ralph de Blancminster established by Edward I at Ennor
        Castle, St. Mary's. The islands assumed special importance
        as they were on the sea route to the English possessions
        around Bordeaux.

1337   The Isles of Scilly included in the Duchy of Cornwall and
        given to the Black Prince.

1342   " Sack " of Scilly by Welsh troops.

1484   Value of the isles, in peace time, forty shillings; in war-
        nothing.

1536—40 Leland's description of the islands. Castle Ennor
        neglected and the islands became a prey to marauders.

1539   The monasteries were dissolved, including Tavistock.

1549   Bill of Attainder against Lord Seymour.

1571   Queen Elizabeth leased the islands to Francis Godolphin.

1593   Star Castle was constructed on " The Hugh " (Hoe) to
        prevent the islands being used as a base by Spain, at war
        with England till 1604.

1623   Prince Charles, afterwards Charles I, stayed on St. Mary's
        for four days.

1637—1681 Star Castle used as a prison for various offenders—
        Dr. Bastwick (1637), John Biddle (1655), and " Seven
        Popish Priests " (1681).

1647   Prince Charles, afterwards Charles II, and his suite, with
        Lords Hopton, Capel, Colepeper, and Sir Edward Hyde,
        took refuge for six weeks at Star Castle after the disastrous
        retreat from the battle of Bodmin. They escaped to the
        Island of Jersey, and the Isles of Scilly surrendered to
        Parliament.

1647—51 Rebellion of Scilly. Star Castle became, in the hands
        of the Royalists under Sir John Grenville, a dangerous nest
        of privateers; passing ships were plundered, regardless of
        nationality.

1651   Holland declared war on the Isles of Scilly. The Dutch
        Admiral Van Tromp arrived off Scilly with twelve men-
        of-war, but was forestalled by Admiral Blake with a
        a Parliamentary fleet.
            The Parliamentary army landed on Tresco and its
        batteries commanded the Roadstead. Subsequently,
        lacking supplies, Sir John Grenville and 1,500 men and
        " officers enough to head an army ", surrendered.

1684   Kelp-ash making introduced. (Kelp is an alkali of value to glass makers, soap manufacturers, and bleachers—it was obtained by burning seaweed).

1707   Sir Cloudesley Shovel, in the *Association*, and four other ships of the fleet (*Eagle, Romsey, Firebrand,* and *Phoenix*) wrecked on the Western Rocks; 2000 men lost their lives.

1742   "The Hugh" completely surrounded with immensely strong fortifications and bastions; the garrison gateway is of this period.

1742—1835   Very poor living for inhabitants (fishing, smuggling and kelp-making).

1823   A market established in St. Mary's.

1835   Augustus Smith obtained lease of the islands from the Crown and became Lord Proprietor. The prosperity of the islands dates from the arrival of this energetic and far-seeing Hertfordshire squire. Augustus Smith built a house near the site of the old monastery on Tresco, and laid out the Abbey Gardens. He also built schools and made education compulsory.

1835—71   Ship-building became an important industry. The Scillonians not only made stout sailing vessels, but manned and owned them. At one time there were five ship-building yards on St. Mary's and the harbour was often full of vessels.

1849   The first Bishop Rock lighthouse constructed.

1855   Samson evacuated by order of the Governor, probably because the inhabitants were too old to man the fishing boats and support themselves.

1859   The Bishop Rock lighthouse rebuilt—the original one was destroyed in a gale in 1850 before it was completed.

1870   (*Period*). St. Agnes became the home of many pilots who boarded the vessels passing the Scillies for the Irish Sea and Bristol and English Channels.

1870   Telegraph company formed by some Scillonians to lay the first cable to the mainland.

1872   Augustus Smith died and was succeeded by his nephew, Lieut. T. Smith-Dorrien, who reversed the name to Dorrien-Smith.

1875   *Schiller* wrecked on Retarrier Ledges.

1880   The start of the flower industry. The original bulbs are said to have been introduced by the Benedictine monks, but Scilly Whites may have been indigenous. It was not until the fashion for buying cut flowers developed in mid-Victorian times, that an experimental hat-box of flowers was despatched from Scilly to Covent Garden.

1891   A new system of local government inaugurated.

1900—1905   Strong gun emplacements constructed on " The Hugh ". The work was abandoned after a quarter of a million pounds had been spent on a plan to make the islands a naval base.

1910   Atlantic liner *Minnehaha*, 13,400 tons, struck on Scilly Rock and later refloated.

1914—18   During the " U "-boat campaign the islands, situated near the main shipping lanes, assumed great strategic importance. A seaplane base was established in Scilly.

1918   Major A. A. Dorrien-Smith, D.S.O., succeeded his father, Lieut. T. Dorrien-Smith, as Governor.

1920   Lease of all inhabited islands, except Tresco, relinquished.

1937   First air service to Scilly. The golf course served as a landing strip.

1939—1945   Following the fall of France the Scillies were heavily manned and fortified. They received frequent attention from enemy aircraft. They were the recipients of much machine-gun fire and about two hundred bombs. A flight of Hurricanes and two air-sea rescue launches were stationed at St. Mary's. The islands became a centre of activity against the hostile submarines—one of which was claimed by the Western Rocks, and another by the Wolf Rock when, hoping to avoid air attack, the " U "-boat approached too near the lighthouse and was wrecked, the crew surrendering to the three keepers.

1954   Income Tax introduced to Scilly for the first time.

1955   On the death of Major A. A. Dorrien-Smith, his son, Lt.-Cdr. T. Dorrien-Smith, R.N. (retd.) succeeded to the lease of Tresco and the uninhabited islands—which are included in the parish of Tresco.

1964   The helicopter service started.

BIBLIOGRAPHY

1222 *Heimskringla* (Translated by Morris and Magnússon, 1891–95, in Saga Library— for Olaf Tryggvason's connection with Scilly) - - - - - - Snorri Sturluson

1478 *Itinerary* - - - - - - William of Worcester

1533—1552 *Itinerary* (published 1710) - - John Leland (Ed. Toulmin Smith 1906–10)

1602 *A Survey of Cornwall* - - - - Richard Carew

1646 *A Relation of the Surrender* - - - John Haslock

1651 *A True Account of the late Reducement of the Isles of Scilly* - - - - - Jos. Lereck

1669 *Travels of Cosmo The Third, Grand Duke of Tuscany, through England in the reign of Charles II* - - - - - Lorenzo Magalotti (Eng. translation 1821)

1676 *Memoirs of Lady Fanshawe* (published 1829) Lady Fanshawe

1702 *S. Devon with a Description of the Scilly Islands* - - - - - - C. S. Ward

1750 *A Natural and Historical Account of the Isles of Scilly* - - - - - Robert Heath

1753 *Of the great alterations which the Isles of Scilly have undergone since the time of the Ancients.* (Philosophical Transactions) Dr. William Borlase

1754 *Antiquities of the County of Cornwall* - Dr. William Borlase

1756 *Observations on the Ancient and Present State of the Islands of Scilly* - - - Dr. William Borlase

1756 *Reviews of Borlase's Book* (In Literary Magazine) - - - - - Samuel Johnson

1794 *A Survey of the Ancient and Present State of the Scilly Isles* - - - - - Rev. John Troutbeck

1804 *A History of Cornwall* (with supplement by Whitaker) - - - - Rev. R. Polwhele

1810 *The Report of the Surveyor General of the Duchy of Cornwall concerning the Formation of a Safe and Capacious Roadstead within the Islands of Scilly* - - Benjamin Tucker

1810 *The Climate of the Isles of Scilly* - - T. T. Macklin

1811 *Observations on the Tin Trade of the Ancients in Cornwall* - - - - - Sir Christopher Hawkins

1814 *Magna Britannia* (vol 3) - - - Lyson

1816 *A History of Cornwall* - - - - Fortescue Hitchens and Samuel Drew

1817	*Historical Survey of the County of Cornwall* (vol. 3) – – – – – – –	C. S. Gilbert
1818	*The Extreme Miseries of the off-islands* –	George C. Smith
1822	*A View of the Present State of the Scilly Islands*	Rev. George Woodley
1824	*A Guide to Mount's Bay and Land's End* (By a Physician) – – – – –	J. A. Paris
1828	*The Scilly Islands and the Famine* – –	G. C. Smith
1834	*The Cornish Tourist* – – – –	Anon.
1841	*Narrative of the Loss of the Steamer "Thames" on the Rocks of Scilly* – – –	Rev. George Woodley
1845	*A Guide to Penzance and its Neighbourhood including the Islands of Scilly* – –	J. S. Courtney
1848	*Thirteen Years Stewardship of the Islands of Scilly* – – – – – –	Augustus Smith
1849	*Sketches in the Scilly Isles* – – –	Lady Sophia Tower
1850	*At the Scilly Isles.* (Argosy vols. 17 and 18)	C. W. Wood
1850	*A Week in the Isles of Scilly* (revised by L. H. Courtney in 1867) – – –	Rev. I. W. North
1850	*Geology of the Isles of Scilly* – – –	J. Carne
1852	*Scilly and its Legends* – – – –	Rev. H. J. Whitfield
1855	*A Londoner's Walk to Land's End and a Tour of the Scilly Islands* – – –	Walter White
1857	*The Beautiful Isles of Britain* – – –	W. Cooper Dendry
1858	*Seaside Studies at Ilfracombe, Tenby, the Scilly Isles, and Jersey* – – –	G. H. Lewes
1859	*Geology of the Isles of Scilly* (in Geologist)	Statham
1861	*Rambles in Western Cornwall* – –	J. C. Halliwell
1861	*Excursions in County of Cornwall, etc.* –	J. C. Halliwell
1861	*Rambles beyond Railways* – – –	Wilkie Collins
	Lyonesse (revisited) – – – –	Tonkin and Row
1863	*The Cassiterides* – – – – –	George Smith
1865	*Yachting Round the West of England* –	Rev. A. G. L'Estrange
1865	*Cornwall and its Coasts* – – –	Alphonse Esquiros
1868	*Vast Sinkings of Lands* – – –	R. A. Peacock
1868	*Sevenstones Lightship* – – – –	Augustus Smith
1869	*Ornithology of Cornwall and Scilly* – –	E. H. Rodd
1869	*Down Channel* – – – – –	R. T. McMullen
1870	*Agriculture of the Scilly Isles.* (In R.A.S. Journal) – – – – – –	Scott and Rivington
1873	*Scilly and its Emperor* – – – –	" S.F.T."
1873	*Observations on the Current to the West of Scilly* – – – – – –	J. Rennell
1875	*The Scilly Isles* (in Fraser's Magazine) –	H. S. Fagan
1875	*Guide to the Scilly Isles* – – –	J. C. and R. W. Tonkin
1876	*A Botanical Trip to the Scilly Isles* – –	W. Curnow
1878	*The Scilly Isles as a Health Resort.* (Brit. Medical Journal) – – – –	Barham

1880	Birds of Cornwall and the Scilly Islands –	E. H. Rodd
1882	Guide to the Isles of Scilly (new edition) –	J. C. and R.W. Tonkin
1883	The Shipwreck of Sir Cloudesley Shovel –	J. H. Cooke
1883	Sixty-eight Years' Experience on the Scilly Islands – – – – – –	Robert Maybee
1885	Dagonet on our Islands – – –	G. R. Sims
1887	Tourists' Companion – – – –	E. W. Crofts
1890	Cornish Feasts and Folklore – – –	M. A. Courtney
1890	The Progress of the Narcissus Culture in the Isles of Scilly (in the Journal of the Royal Horticultural Society) – – –	T. A. Dorrien-Smith
1891	The Abbots of Tavistock – – –	Rev. D. P. Alford
1870, 1890, 1898	Journal of the Royal Agricultural Society (articles on agriculture in Scilly and the flower industry)	
1893	The Age of the Saints: a Monograph of Early Christianity in Cornwall – –	W. Copeland Borlase
1894	A Summer in the Scilly Islands – –	J. W. White
1895	Guide to Cornwall and the Scilly Isles –	W. H. Tregellas
1896	The Story of Atlantis – – – –	A. P. Sinnett
1897	The Scilly Isles (Newne's Guide) – –	
1897	Faire Lyonesse – – – – –	James G. Owen
1897	Lyonesse (Handbook for Isles of Scilly), (Homeland Handbooks No. 4) – –	J. C. Tonkin and Prescott Row
1899	Book of the West – – – –	Rev. S. Baring-Gould
	The Wolf Rock Lighthouse – – –	J. N. Douglas
1906	Isles of Ictis – – – – –	Emm. Green
1906	History and Geography of Cornwall –	Thurstan C. Peter
1906	Victoria County History of Cornwall	Ed. William Page
1906	The Geology of the Isles of Scilly –	George Barrow
1906	Scilly and the Scillonians – –	J. G. Uren
1909	Cassiterides and Ictis—Where are they?	Thurstan C. Peter
1909	The Romance of Smuggling – –	Rev. Athol Forbes
1909	Cornish Charcters and Strange Events	Rev. S. Baring-Gould
1909	Flora of Cornwall (supplement 1922)	Davey
1910	The Cornish Coast and the Isles of Scilly –	C. G. Harper
1910	The Isles of Scilly – – – –	Jessie Mothersole
1923	Ward Lock's Guide to Penzance and the Scilly Isles	
1924	Wild Nature in Scillonia – – –	C. J. King
1925	The Isles of Scilly – – – –	Alexander G. Gibson and Herbert J. Gibson
	The Godolphins – – – – –	Brigadier F. C. Marsh
1925	The Scillonian (The Quarterly Magazine of the Isles of Scilly No. 1) – – –	
1928	The Quarterly Journal of the Geological Society (for the granites of Scilly) –	C. W. Osman

1929 and 1935 *Proceedings of the Zoological Society*
(for spiders of Scilly)   –   –   –   W. S. Bristowe

1931 *Proceedings of the Zoological Society* (for
beetles of Scilly)   –   –   –   –   K. G. Blair

1925 *The Entomologist* (for insects) –   –   –

1930 *The Entomologist* (for butterflies)   –   –   P. P. Graves

1932 *Cornish Seafarers*   –   –   –   –   A. K. Hamilton Jenkin

1932 *Cornwall and Scilly* (The County Archae-
ologies) –   –   –   –   –   –   H. O'Neill Henken

1933 *Cornwall in the Great Civil War and Inter-
regnum 1642–1660*   –   –   –   –   Mary Coate
King's Popular Guide   –   –   –   –   C. J. King
St. Michael's Mount   –   –   –   –   Rev. T. Taylor

1934 *Isles of the Island*   –   –   –   –   S. P. B. Mais

1935 *St. Samson in Cornwall*   –   –   –   G. E. Doble

1935 *The West Country*   –   –   –   –   R. A. J. Walling

1936 *Beast Book for the Pocket* (on Seals, Dolphins,
Porpoises, Scilly Shrew, etc.) –   –   Edmund Sandars

1937 The Building of Star Castle (In *Old Cornwall*, The Journal of the Federation of
Old Cornwall Societies, Vol. III, No. 2.
Winter 1937, and Vol III, No. 3, Summer 1938 –   –   –   –   –   J. E. Hooper

1938 The Garden Isles of Scilly (in the *National
Geographic Magazine*, Vol. 74, No. 6,
December, 1938)   –   –   –   W. Robert Moore

1938 *Isles of Scilly Guide* (1st edition)   –   E. L. Bowley

1939 and 1940 Notes on the Flora of the Isles of
Scilly (in *Journal of Botany*)   –   J. E. Lousley

1941 *Tudor Cornwall*   –   –   –   A. L. Rowse

1941 The Dual Nature of the Megalithic Colo-
nisation of Prehistoric Europe (in *Proceedings of the Prehistoric Society*)   –   G. E. Daniel

1945 *Cornwall and its People*   –   –   A. K. Hamilton Jenkin

1945 *The Fortunate Islands* (1st edition) –   E. L. Bowley

1945 *St. Martin's, St. Helen's and Tean* –   H. A. Lewis

1946 *The Coastline of England and Wales* (for
geology of Scilly)   –   –   –   J. A. Steers

1947 Tresco under Three Reigns (in *Journal of
Royal Horticultural Society*, 1947)   –   J. W. Hunkin, Bishop of
Truro

1947 *British Lighthouses*   –   –   –   J. P. Bowen

1948 *The Scilly Isles* –   –   –   –   Geoffrey Grigson

1949 *Ancient Monuments of the Isles of Scilly* –   B. H. St. J. O'Neil

1950 *Shipwrecks on the Isles of Scilly*   –   Charlotte Dorrien-Smith

1953 *The Scilly Isles* –   –   –   –   C. C. Vyvyan

1956 *Hobnails and Seaboots*   –   –   –   Wendy Aldridge

1956 *Isles of Flowers*   –   –   –   –   Ernest Kay

1957c. *Isles of Scilly Visitor's Handbook* – – Maxwell Fraser
1957 *Report of St. Agnes Bird Observatory* (and
later editions) – – – – – Ed. J. L. F. Parslaw
1958 *Scilly Isles Survey* – – – – The British Travel and
Holidays Association
1958 *The Lost Land* (underwater exploration) – John Dunbar
1959 *Wrecks of the Isles of Scilly* (Reprinted from
The Mariner's Mirror, vol. 45, No. 4,
Dec. 1959 and Vol. 46 No. 2, May 1960) Juliet du Boulay
1960 *The Isles of Scilly* – – – – G. Forrester Mathews
1960 *Isles of Scilly Visitors' Handbook* – – Ed. G. Sage
1962 *Official Guide to Tresco, Isles of Scilly* – Ann Faber
1963 *Scilly and the Scillonians* (A pictorial
history) – – – – – F. E. Gibson
1964 *The Standard Guide to the Isles of Scilly*
(24th edition) – – – – R. L. Bowley
and also—
1921 *Antiquaries Journal* (on Roman altar)
1933 *Antiquaries Journal* (on megalithic monuments)
1934 *Antiquaries Journal* (on iron-age finds on
Teän
1941 *Antiquaries Journal* (on Celtic monastery on
St. Helen's)
1941 *Antiquaries Journal* (on cliff castles)
1927 *Antiquity* (on Lyonesse) – – – O. G. S. Crawford
1944 *Antiquity* (on megalithic monuments and
Celtic Saints) – – – – – E. G. Bowen

POETRY

Songs of the West – – – – Rev. S. Baring-Gould
1866 *Roathmere and other Poems* – – – Sarah Eliza Tonkin
The Ballad of the Royal Anne – – Crosbie Garstin
1925 *Island Lights* – – – – – Geoffrey Fyson
Lyonesse – – – – – – B. M. Warrand

FICTION

Cornubia – – – – – – G. Woodley
Armorel of Lyonesse – – – – Sir Walter Besant
Major Vigoureux – – – – "Q"(Sir Arthur
Quiller-Couch)
Tom Tiddler's Ground – – – – " Q " (Sir Arthur
Quiller-Couch)
The Dominant Law – – – – D. Lewis
Fairy Gold – – – – – – Sir Compton Mackenzie
Miranda of the Balcony – – – – A. E. W. Mason
The Watchers – – – – – A. E. W. Mason
A Man of Moods – – – – H. D. Lowry

	Bazin's Gold – – – – – E. Cornish
	Wrecked on Scilly – – – – M. Onley
	Lost Land of King Arthur – – – J. C. Waters
	The Watchers on the Longships – – F. J. Cobb
1954	*The Riddle of Samson* – – – – A. Garve
	Dangerous Waters – – – – J. Cox
1913	*Maze of Scilly* – – – – – E. J. Tiddy
	Enter the Saint – – – – – L. Charteris
	Black Gull – – – – – – D. Lamport
1956	*Cat in Gloves* – – – – – Denis Delaney
1959	*Seven Red Roses* – – – – Leila Mackinlay

INDEX